S0-AFN-667

DIALOGUE
OF LOVE

ORTHODOX CHRISTIANITY AND CONTEMPORARY THOUGHT

George E. Demacopoulos
and Aristotle Papanikolaou

SERIES EDITORS

This series consists of books that seek to bring Orthodox Christianity into an engagement with contemporary forms of thought. Its goal is to promote (1) historical studies in Orthodox Christianity that are interdisciplinary, employ a variety of methods, and speak to contemporary issues; and (2) constructive theological arguments in conversation with patristic sources and that focus on contemporary questions ranging from the traditional theological and philosophical themes of God and human identity to cultural, political, economic, and ethical concerns. The books in the series explore both the relevancy of Orthodox Christianity to contemporary challenges and the impact of contemporary modes of thought on Orthodox self-understandings.

DIALOGUE OF LOVE

Breaking the Silence of Centuries

Edited by
John Chryssavgis

Fordham University Press

New York 2014

Copyright © 2014 Fordham University Press

All rights reserved. No part of this publication may be reproduced, stored in a retrieval system, or transmitted in any form or by any means—electronic, mechanical, photocopy, recording, or any other—except for brief quotations in printed reviews, without the prior permission of the publisher.

Fordham University Press has no responsibility for the persistence or accuracy of URLs for external or third-party Internet websites referred to in this publication and does not guarantee that any content on such websites is, or will remain, accurate or appropriate.

Fordham University Press also publishes its books in a variety of electronic formats. Some content that appears in print may not be available in electronic books.

Library of Congress Control Number: 2014933701

Printed in the United States of America
16 15 14   5 4 3 2 1
First edition

Contents

Contents

FOREWORD

Metropolitan John (Zizioulas) of Pergamon

Fifty years ago, the historic meeting of Ecumenical Patriarch Athenagoras and Pope Paul VI in Jerusalem marked the beginning of a new era in the relations between the churches of Rome and Constantinople, and indirectly between Roman Catholicism and Orthodoxy as a whole. The significance of this event can be fully appreciated only if placed against the background of a millennium branded with mutual mistrust, theological polemic, and, above all, estrangement between the two great traditions of the Church. In the words of the late Father Georges Florovsky, these traditions are likened to conjoined sisters unable to be separated from each other without inflicting serious damage to both. And, indeed, by following their separate and independent ways for a thousand years, the East and the West have run the risk of damaging the Body of Christ by acquiring a sense of self-sufficiency that was absent from the consciousness of the ancient Church, which had always felt the need to seek and secure agreement on matters of faith through ecumenical councils comprising both the East and the West.

East, where is thy West? West, where is thy East? These questions were demanding an answer, and the Jerusalem meeting of the two Church leaders fifty years ago came as a first step toward recovering the lost relationship.

"Having sought to meet one another, we have together found the Lord . . . indicating the way to follow," Patriarch Athenagoras said to the Pope when they met in the Holy City. And the Pope replied: "No doubt, from the one side as well as from the other, the roads leading to union may be long and sown with difficulties. But the two paths converge the one with the other and lead to the sources of the Gospel." The East and the West have followed separate ways since the eleventh century but they must be reminded that they have a common history of Scripture and Tradition behind them, to which they can go back in order to find common ground for the future.

The meeting in Jerusalem was only the beginning of a long journey, which the succeeding generations were called to continue. Looking back at the fifty years after the event, we can be grateful to our Lord that a great deal has been achieved both in the dialogue of love and in the dialogue of truth. The spirit of fraternal love and mutual respect has replaced the old polemic and suspicion. At the theological level, important common documents have been produced by the Joint International Commission of the Theological Dialogue of the two Churches. But there is still a lot to be achieved and, indeed, the path seems to be long. This path, however, must be followed in spite of difficulties; there is no alternative. To discontinue and let brambles overtake the path would mean a return to an estranged past from which the meeting at Jerusalem wanted to liberate us.

Reflecting upon the meeting of Pope Francis and Ecumenical Patriarch Bartholomew in Jerusalem (May 2014), we expect from it a strong symbolic confirmation of the will to continue the path the two great Church leaders inaugurated half a century ago in the same spirit of love and faithfulness to the truth of the Gospel, as this was transmitted to us by the great Fathers of the Church. The use and abuse of religion for political and other secular purposes; the difficulties facing Christians all over the world, and particularly in the areas where the Christian Church was born and grew up, regardless of confessional identities; the injustices inflicted on the weak members of contemporary societies; and the alarming ecological crisis that threatens the integrity and the very survival of God's creation—all these call for common action and the solution of the problems still dividing us. Today, even more than fifty years ago, there is an urgent need for reconciliation, and this renders the meeting of Pope Francis and Ecumenical Patriarch Bartholomew in Jerusalem (May 2014) an event of great significance.

PREFACE

◇◇◇◇◇◇◇◇◇◇◇◇◇◇◇◇

John Chryssavgis

In 1964, a little-noticed, albeit pioneering encounter in the Holy Land between the heads of the Roman Catholic Church and the Orthodox Church spawned numerous contacts and diverse openings between these two sister churches, which had not communicated with one another for centuries.

When Ecumenical Patriarch Bartholomew took the unprecedented step of attending the inaugural mass of Pope Francis on March 19, 2013—something that had never occurred in the 2,000-year history of the Christian Church—he proposed that the two leaders meet in 2014 in the Holy Land in observation of the events in 1964. Thus, five decades later, Pope Francis and Patriarch Bartholomew meet in Jerusalem to commemorate that historical event and celebrate the closer relations that have emerged and developed through mutual exchanges of formal visits as well as an official international theological dialogue that began in 1980.

The first two chapters in this book explore the historical perspectives of what occurred during that "pilgrimage toward unity" on January 5–6, 1964, as well as the preliminary steps toward theological dialogue, both internationally and in the United States of America, as a result of the dialogue of love.

John Chryssavgis

I am indebted to Fr. Brian E. Daley, S.J., for his contribution, and especially for his vital role in the ongoing theological dialogue between the Roman Catholic and Orthodox Churches in North America. The final chapter is a hitherto unpublished translation of an insightful reflection by the late Fr. Georges Florovsky (1893–1979), perhaps the most prominent and influential Orthodox theologian of the twentieth century, on the importance and implications of that meeting between Ecumenical Patriarch Athenagoras and Pope Paul VI. I am thankful to Rev. Matthew Baker for translating and making this text available for publication. The foreword by Metropolitan John [Zizioulas] of Pergamon and afterword by Walter Cardinal Kasper provide a fitting homage by two distinguished hierarchs and theologians, both of whom have been instrumental in the Joint International Commission of the Theological Dialogue between the two Churches.

Dialogue of Love: Breaking the Silence of Centuries is a tribute to Athenagoras and Paul VI, who dared and risked sharing an encounter and embarking on a journey that shattered the silence and arrogance of past divisions. They recognized the responsibility of their apostolic inheritance as successors of Andrew and Peter, the first called among Christ's disciples. They understood the accountability of their pastoral leadership for the generations to come. As "good shepherds, they went on ahead before their sheep" (John 10:4). And they chose rapprochement over estrangement, reconciliation over alienation, and loving unity over bitter dissension. While the journey continues, despite obstacles, nevertheless that whispering sound in 1964 has resounded "like the rush of a mighty wind" (Acts 2:2) over the last fifty years. And in May 2014, somewhere near that "upper room," the vision of unity will be reaffirmed and revitalized.

I would like to express my gratitude to the Rev. Joseph M. McShane, S.J., president of Fordham University, who promptly and spontaneously accepted the request of the V. Rev. Alexander Karloutsos to publish this book in recognition of this historical event. Fredric Nachbaur (director) and Eric Newman (managing editor) at Fordham University Press were, once again, very gracious and accommodating. I have always enjoyed working with them. Finally, to my editor, Marilyn Rouvelas, I profess my unremitting appreciation.

1

PILGRIMAGE TOWARD UNITY

Ecumenical Patriarch Athenagoras
and Pope Paul VI in Jerusalem
Based on Correspondence and Archives

◇◇◇◇◇◇◇◇◇◇◇◇◇◇

John Chryssavgis

In January 1964, two Christian prelates broke a silence of centuries with a simple gesture of embrace and a few gentle words. A little-noticed historic meeting in Jerusalem between Ecumenical Patriarch Athenagoras and Pope Paul VI reflected the simple dominical prayer and commandment by Christ that His disciples "all may be one" (John 17:21); but what began was a journey of exceptional transformation in the relations between the Roman Catholic and Orthodox Churches, two sister churches that had shared an entire millennium of common doctrine and spiritual tradition, followed by an entire millennium of division and alienation.

Before the two prelates met, the Ecumenical Patriarch would wittily—albeit at once so tragically and truthfully, mystically and realistically—respond to reporters asking about the purpose of their meeting: "I came here to say 'good morning' to my beloved brother, the Pope. You must remember that it has been five hundred and twenty-five years since we have spoken to one another!"[1] At the dawn of a new era of positive relations between the Roman Catholic and Orthodox Churches, Athenagoras's spur-of-the-moment prophesy echoes Maya Angelou's celebrated poetry:

> Here, on the pulse of this new day
> You may have the grace to look up and out
> . . . And into your brother's face
> . . . And say simply
> Very simply
> With hope—
> Good morning.[2]

Thus it was that, in the brief space of less than forty-eight hours, January 5–6, 1964, His Holiness the late Pope Paul commenced a historical visit to the Holy Land, establishing a tradition subsequently honored by his successors. It was the first time a Roman pontiff had traveled abroad for over a century, the first time a Roman pontiff flew in an airplane, and the first time a Roman pontiff visited Jerusalem.

1. In the biography of Patriarch Athenagoras by Demetrios Tsakonas, *A Man Sent by God: The Life of Patriarch Athenagoras* (Brookline, Mass.: Holy Cross Orthodox Press, 1977), 56.
2. Maya Angelou, "On the Pulse of Morning" (New York: Random House, 1993).

The Pope's journey, however, was much more than a pilgrimage to the Holy Land, the focal point of reverence and travel for adherents of all the Abrahamic faiths. Christian leaders and faithful have visited Jerusalem since at least the fourth century, encouraged by the holy Emperor Constantine and his saintly mother Helen, recognizing its association with the early apostles, saints, and martyrs but most especially its significance as the place where God's feet once walked when His Word assumed flesh and dwelt among us. So, too, Pope Paul traveled to Bethlehem (where Christ was born), Nazareth (where Christ grew up), and Jerusalem (where Christ died and rose).

Nevertheless, the "pilgrim Pope" was also the "ecumenical Pope" inasmuch as his historical visit was a unique occasion for an extraordinary and pioneering encounter with Ecumenical Patriarch Athenagoras. Following in the footsteps of his predecessor, not only did Pope Paul bring a successful conclusion to the revolutionary Second Vatican Council in 1965, but he also brought to fruition and realization the ecumenical overture to the Orthodox Christian Church.

Thus, on January 5, 1964, Pope Paul VI met with Ecumenical Patriarch Athenagoras on the Mount of Olives. It was the first time the Western pontiff and the Eastern primate—the universal leader of the Western Church and the spiritual leader of the Eastern Church, the Pope of Rome and the Archbishop of New Rome—met face-to-face since 1438 at the Council of Florence. And the venue for the encounter was the Mount of Olives, the very place where our Lord Jesus Christ, the Great

High Priest, addressed His Father on the night of His betrayal for the unity of His followers, boldly and passionately praying that His disciples may be one, *ut unum sint* (John 17:21).

First Steps to Transformation

Prior to this groundbreaking meeting of the two prelates fifty years ago, for many centuries the Eastern and Western Churches were not in formal contact and shared very little official communication, especially after what became known as the Great Schism of 1054. There were two brief occasions of encounter and dialogue regarding reunification during the thirteenth and fifteenth centuries, but these left behind feelings of bitterness rather than hopefulness, at least for the Orthodox Christians of the East. The estrangement was of course markedly accentuated and apparent after the tragic events of the Crusades in the late twelfth and early thirteenth centuries.

Mindful of this extraordinary and even bitter history, Patriarch Athenagoras commissioned the newly elected Archbishop Iakovos of North and South America in 1959 to travel to Rome in order to meet with the "charismatic" and "angelic"—as he was widely known[3]—Pope John XXIII, who had just months earlier announced the convocation of the Second Vatican Council that later began in 1962. When Iakovos visited the Pope on March 17, 1959, it was the first encounter be-

---

3. See Evangelos Theodorou, "The Contribution of Ecumenical Patriarch Athenagoras to the Reconciliation of Fraternal Relations between the Orthodox and Roman Catholic Churches," in *Athenagoras I: Ecumenical Patriarch*, ed. I. Anastasiou (Ioannina: Society of Epirotic Studies, 1975), 312.

tween a representative of the Patriarch and the Pope of Rome since May 1547; only one month later, a representative from the Vatican would visit the Phanar to meet with Patriarch Athenagoras.[4]

Then, in the middle of the twentieth century, Athenagoras—formerly Archbishop of North and South America and then Ecumenical Patriarch, a man committed to the fullness of truth and convinced of the ecumenical mandate of the Orthodox Church—undertook the inspiring, albeit daring, initiative of writing a personal letter to Pope John XXIII on May 30, 1963, wishing him a speedy recovery from illness, a simple gesture of concern between two individuals.[5] It was the first time in some four hundred years that either a Pope or a Patriarch communicated directly with his counterpart. In personal conversations, Patriarch Athenagoras often spoke of the same Pope, adapting the opening words of the Gospel of John: "There was a man sent from God whose name was John" (John 1:6). In a letter addressed to Patriarch Athenagoras on

4. See E. J. Stormon, *Towards the Healing of Schism: The Sees of Rome and Constantinople (1958–1984)* (Mahwah, N.J.: Paulist Press, 1987), 9.

5. Communications and correspondence between the Vatican and the Phanar are translated directly from the official volume edited by a mixed commission comprising Archim. Damaskinos Papandreou and Archim. Bartholomew Archontonis (currently the Ecumenical Patriarch), as well as Père Pierre Duprey and Père Christophe Dumont, *Tomos Agapis: Vatican-Phanar (1958–1970)* (Rome and Istanbul, 1971). Translations of the *Volume of Charity* also containing certain supplementary items appeared in Spanish (Madrid: Biblioteca de Autores Cristianos, 1973), German (Vienna: Pro Oriente, 1978), and French (Paris: Cerf "Semeurs," 1984). An augmented English edition and translation is available: Stormon, *Towards the Healing of Schism*.

December 30, 1963, as well as in his response to the Ecumenical Patriarch on the Mount of Olives on January 6, 1964, Pope Paul VI recalled the Patriarch's application of these words to John XXIII and referred to it as "a flash of intuition."

After a letter signed by Metropolitan Maximos of Sardis in the name of Ecumenical Patriarch Athenagoras, congratulating Pope Paul VI on his election and new "ministry in the sacred and sister Church of Rome, for the advancement of the spirit of unity within the Christian world" (September 9, 1963), the Pope responded in what was the first handwritten letter from a Pope to an Ecumenical Patriarch since 1584,[6] acknowledging his commitment "to contribute toward the restoration of complete unity among Christians" (September 20, 1963). In turn, the Ecumenical Patriarchate published the papal letter in its official bulletin under the title "The Two Sister Churches," the first modern use of an ancient expression originated by St. Ignatius of Antioch and describing relations between the Churches of Rome and Constantinople; the same terminology would also enter the vocabulary of the Second Vatican Council.

Upon learning of the announcement of the imminent visit of Pope Paul VI to the Holy Land on January 6, 1964, Patriarch Athenagoras preached on December 6, 2013, to a large congregation in a church of a local Istanbul neighborhood,

6. In 1584, Pope Gregory XIII communicated with Patriarch Jeremiah II about the reform of the calendar; the new (Gregorian) calendar was formally instituted in 1582.

where he was celebrating the Divine Liturgy for the feast day of St. Nicholas, and joyfully explained the significance of this visit, observing that "it would be an act of divine providence if, on the occasion of the papal journey, the heads of all the holy Churches of Christ, in the East and West alike, of the three major Confessions, were together to express contrition . . . tears . . . and prayers for the reconciliation of all people in accordance with His will."[7] On December 14, 1963, Patriarch Athenagoras communicated with all heads of the autocephalous Orthodox Churches to inform them of his decision to go to Jerusalem;[8] most of these Churches responded positively.[9]

7. The spontaneous reaction by Athenagoras, as well as his express desire for leaders of the Orthodox, Roman Catholic, and Anglican Churches to meet together in the hope and prayer of reconciliation, demonstrates the openness of his heart and mind. In the end, it was only the leaders of the Orthodox and Roman Catholic Churches that met in Jerusalem. Also cited in the formal announcement from the Chief Secretariat of the Ecumenical Patriarchate, dated December 6, 1963, which however omits the phrase "of the three major Confessions." A few days later, on December 10, 1963, Mgr. Pierre Duprey (1922–2007), then Undersecretary of the Secretariat for Christian Unity (newly founded in 1960 by Pope John XXIII), visited Patriarch Athenagoras to provide details of the papal journey to the Holy Land. From the minutes of the Chief Secretary at the Phanar, dated January 11, 1963.

8. Aristeides Panotis observes that this communication was for the most part a conventional notification, rather than a request for consent. See Panotis, *Paul VI and Athenagoras I: Peacemakers* (Athens: Dragan Institute of Europe, 1971), in Greek. Panotis adds that congratulatory letters were received from the Patriarchs of Antioch and Moscow, Serbia and Romania, the Archbishop of Cyprus, and other Orthodox Churches.

9. The report by Metropolitan Athenagoras to the Holy and Sacred Synod in Constantinople, dated January 3, 1964, notes the negative stance and vehement

John Chryssavgis

Nonetheless, while extraordinary, this admission was not in fact exceptional. In a letter dated January 14, 1964, to the clergy and laity of his archdiocese, "describing the momentous meeting" of the two prelates in Jerusalem only days earlier, Archbishop Iakovos of North and South America and Canada observed, "Already as early as 1949, namely since the time that he ascended the Ecumenical Throne of Constantinople, His All-Holiness our Patriarch, expressed his desire to meet personally with the Roman pontiff. He later repeated this desire to Pope John XXIII, the successor to Pope Pius XII. Finally, he expressed the same desire in person in the Church of St. Nicholas at Cibali (Constantinople) on December 6, the

---

opposition of the Patriarchate of Moscow to the preparations and forthcoming meeting in Jerusalem between the Pope and the Ecumenical Patriarch, as these criticisms appeared in the Italian newspaper *Il Tempo*, claiming that the event was political in nature. In his report, Metropolitan Athenagoras highlighted his response to journalists about the "spiritual nature" of the event, which "has no political motive. Any other journalistic suspicions cannot in any way shake the absolute unity and cooperation on matters of faith among sister Orthodox Churches because what unites them is not politics, but faith and their common concern for the promotion and protection of its integrity. The encounter between the Pope and the Patriarch has a merely spiritual character inasmuch as both leaders are traveling to venerate and meet at the empty tomb, which remains a manifestation of Christ's victory." The media was in general very favorable about the encounter in Jerusalem, which led Patriarch Athenagoras to issue a communiqué on January 22, 1964, after the conclusion of the journey to the Holy Land, expressing his "warm gratitude for the contribution of the local and international press, both daily and periodical as well as television and radio in promoting this historical event and informing public opinion." From the archives of the Chief Secretariat at the Phanar.

day after it was announced that Paul VI would make a pilgrimage to the Holy Land."[10]

Only days, then, after this spontaneous and inspired expression, Ecumenical Patriarch Athenagoras assigned two representatives (Metropolitans Meliton of Ilioupolis and Theira, and Athenagoras of Thyateira [Great Britain]) to visit the Vatican, where in an address to the Pope, Metropolitan Athenagoras noted that "perhaps it is a matter of divine inspiration that on the one hand Pope Paul and on the other Patriarch Athenagoras were ascending the mountain of the Lord, while Christians throughout the world were praying that the two might meet at the summit of this mountain. . . . Peter and Andrew were brothers. Yet, for centuries they have not communicated with one another. Behold, now they are revealing a mutual desire and wish for exchange and encounter. This wish is none other than the Lord's command and the Christian people's nostalgia" (December 28, 1963). Pope Paul VI responded in writing to the Ecumenical Patriarch, stating that the Patriarch's words "struck a profound chord in his heart" and that "any impediments arising from process and details are dispersed by the common desire for encounter. For wherever the divine Spirit and God's love prevail, truly all challenges may be overcome" (December 30, 1963).

The same patriarchal delegates were also to meet with papal representatives in order, as per the written request by Patriarch

---

10. Demetrios Constantelos, ed., *Encyclicals and Documents of the Greek Orthodox Archdiocese of North and South America* (Thessaloniki: Patriarchal Institute for Patristic Studies, 1976), 788–89. My translation.

Athenagoras to finalize the details of the imminent meeting in Jerusalem.[11] In the official report to the Holy and Great Synod, dated January 3, 1964, Metropolitan Athenagoras of Thyateira (Great Britain) recorded his meetings with Cardinal Cicognani of the Vatican's department for external affairs.[12] Pope Paul personally conveyed his wish that the Lord's Prayer and the seventeenth chapter of St. John's Gospel with Christ's prayer for the Apostles be recited in Greek and Latin during the encounter in the Holy Lands. During his brief stay in Rome, Archbishop Athenagoras celebrated the Divine Liturgy at the Greek Orthodox Church of St. Andrew on Sunday, December 29, 1963, where the serving deacon was Fr. Bartholomew, current Ecumenical Patriarch.[13]

The Melting Away of Silence

Thus ensued the historic meeting of the Pope and the Patriarch in Jerusalem on January 5, 1964,[14] an encounter and event

11. The personal letter from the Patriarch to the Pope (Prot. No. 1084, dated December 26, 1963, patriarchal archives), was read aloud in Greek by the Pope upon receiving it in his hands. Among the agreed details for the imminent encounter, signed in Rome on December 30, 1963, was an exchange of meetings between the Pope and Patriarch Benedictos of Jerusalem, which took place on January 5 and 6, 1964.

12. Metropolitan Meliton of Ilioupolis and Theira was finally unable to travel to Rome inasmuch as he was not given the necessary permit to leave Turkey in order to participate in the patriarchal delegation and the meetings with the papal representatives, which took place December 28–30, 1963.

13. In the official report preserved in the Chief Secretariat at the Phanar.

14. The Ecumenical Patriarch and his entourage traveled from Rhodes to Jerusalem on January 5, 1964, in a private plane provided by Aristotle Onassis.

that was truly remarkable and momentous, albeit somewhat unexpected and unplanned. This was the first time in some 525 years—and only the second time in well over 1,000, possibly even 1,900 years—that an Ecumenical Patriarch was meeting face-to-face with a Roman pontiff. At the Council of Florence in 1438–39, Archbishop Joseph II of Constantinople met with Pope Eugene IV on March 8, 1438; the Patriarch was in attendance for most of the conciliar sessions, although he died in the final days of the council. During the previous effort toward reconciliation of the two Churches, at the Council of Lyons in 1274, Ecumenical Patriarch Joseph was not in attendance; indeed, that entire gathering was more a political than an ecclesiastical event, orchestrated by the Roman Pope in association with the Byzantine Emperor. Prior to the twentieth century, in fact, there were very few, if any face-to-face meetings between the two leaders of the Eastern and Western Churches.[15]

On the same day, prior to departing for Jerusalem, after the Divine Liturgy, Patriarch Athenagoras held a memorial service in honor of the late President John F. Kennedy, who had died on November 20, 1963. At the airport in Jerusalem, the Patriarch was met by King Hussein of Jordan and Patriarch Benedictos of Jerusalem. In addition to prelates and archons of the Phanar and professors G. Konidaris, P. Chrestou, and D. Tsakonas, the patriarchal entourage included Archbishop Iakovos of America and Archbishop Ezekiel of Australia. From the official report by members of the patriarchal entourage, submitted to the Holy and Sacred Synod on January 20, 1964, upon their return from Jerusalem.

15. For example, only once did a Pope attend an ecumenical council: Pope Vigilius was present during the Fifth Ecumenical Council, held in Constantinople in 553, but he was actually in the city under house arrest. I am grateful to Prof. George Demacopoulos of Fordham University for this information.

Diplomatic encounters between the two sees were almost always enacted through representatives.

The announcement of the encounter took most people by surprise, including well-intentioned theological analysts.[16] For instance, the renowned historian Fr. Georges Florovsky underlined an "ecumenism in time" (as a discernment by the various Christian denominations of a common background in the apostolic tradition) rather than an "ecumenism in space" (as an agreement by Christian confessions as they are), emphasizing a "reintegration of mind" rather than a mere reconciliation of actions.[17] After all, "as the late Fr. Georges Florovsky liked to repeat, the authentic catholicity of the Church must include both East and West."[18] Thus, with regard to the meeting in

---

16. There were also a good number of ill-intentioned scholars, such as Konstantinos Mouratidis, Professor of Canon Law at the University of Athens; see Mouratidis, *The Ecumenical Movement: The Contemporary Great Temptation of Orthodoxy* (Athens, 1973). On the other side, Prof. Nikos Nissiotis claimed that Patriarch Athenagoras "only offended theologians, whose work is restricted to an infertile repetition of scholastic formulations, who are confined to hiding behind monolithic dogmatisms, who are isolated from life, and unrelated to people's expectations." See Nissiotis, "Athenagoras: Ecumenical Patriarch for All People and All Churches," in *Apostolos Titos* (Herakleion Crete, 1972), 9, in Greek.

17. See Georges Florovsky, "The Orthodox Churches and the Ecumenical Movement Prior to 1910," in *Christianity and Culture* (Belmont, Mass.: Nordland, 1974), esp. 29, 78. Also see Georges Florovsky, "Primitive Tradition and the Traditions," in *The Unity We Seek*, ed. William S. Morris (Toronto: Ryerson Press, 1962), 28–38.

18. [Metropolitan] John Zizioulas [of Pergamon], *Being as Communion: Studies in Personhood and the Church* (Crestwood, N.Y.: St. Vladimir's Seminary Press, 1985), introduction.

Jerusalem five decades ago, Fr. Florovsky noted: "In any case, the meeting of the patriarchs was an unexpected event, almost a surprise. Few were prepared for it inwardly, psychologically and spiritually, even among those who were ready to welcome it sincerely." While some embraced it with joy, as a favorable sign, for others it was troubling, causing alarm and suspicion. However, for the more moderate and discerning, including Florovsky himself, "the Palestinian meeting of the Patriarchs—of the new and the old Rome, for a long time and still divided—[was] a timely *reminder*, and a double reminder: of the fact of separation, and of the task of unity. A reminder and *a call*."[19]

Archbishop Iakovos, a confidant and coworker of the Ecumenical Patriarch, was less fearful and more hopeful in his "personal impressions and comments about the significance of the historic meeting": "The full import of the meetings on January 5th and 6th will not be revealed until much later. No one can know at present what these two prelates exchanged in their private conversations, what thoughts they shared with one another, or if they came to some agreement on what the two churches of the East and West should do in the near or more distant future. . . . I have, however, every reason to believe that their encounter was a meeting *in Christ* and a mutual outpouring of spirit and soul in His presence."[20]

19. Originally published in Russian as "Знамение Пререкаемо," *Вестник Русского Студенческого Христианского Движения*, nos. 72–73, I–II, 1964, 1–7. See chapter 3, this volume.

20. Constantelos, *Encyclicals and Documents of the Greek Orthodox Archdiocese of North and South America*, 789. My translation.

On January 5, 1964, at 9:30 p.m., the first contact was held in the Apostolic Delegation residence on the magnificent Mount of Olives, where the Pope awaited and received the Patriarch. The two leaders embraced one another in a gracious historical gesture that—to quote the official report submitted subsequently to the Holy and Sacred Synod on January 20, 1964—"melted away centuries of silence between their respective Churches. A milestone and the dawn of a new Christendom was consecrated at that moment, when the attention of the entire Christian world was focused on the City of love and reconciliation, while the hearts of all well-intentioned people were beating in anticipation as they waited to hear the message of unity and fraternity in Christ." As they entered the formal reception hall hand in hand, the Pope took the throne on the left and signaled to the Patriarch to be seated on an identical throne on the right.

There followed a fourteen-minute private meeting, during which the two prelates understood that "it would take a long time for the wealth of impressions and emotions to be fully articulated." They promised to "deal openly with one another, to speak their minds honestly, to express their thoughts about the constitution of the church, even if one has evolved differently to the other in two or three points of doctrine." At the same time, both leaders recognized that they were faced with "a difficult task because of people's mentality and psychology," which would resist their ecumenical openings. Nonetheless, they pledged not to allow "questions of prestige and primacy, or matters related to discipline, honor, privilege and ambition" to interfere with their goal "to discern the truth," but rather "to cherish the church" (Athenagoras) and "to serve" (Paul VI).[21]

Immediately afterward, the entourages of the two leaders were invited into the main hall,[22] where Patriarch Athenagoras addressed the Pope in Greek (a French translation was read by the chief secretary of the Ecumenical Patriarchate); the Pope responded in French, addressing the assembly in a personal tone and offering a golden chalice to the Patriarch as a symbol of the unity that they seek in common. The first meeting concluded with the recital of the Lord's Prayer in Greek and Latin.

A second meeting was held at 10 a.m. on the following day, January 6, 1964, in the summer residence of the Patriarch of Jerusalem on the momentous Mount of Olives, where upon his return from Bethlehem Pope Paul visited Patriarch Athenagoras. It is on this sacred mountain ridge—famous from the time of Alexander the Great in the fourth century B.C.E.—that prophets are buried, where Jesus wept over Jerusalem (Luke 19:41) and regularly withdrew for prayer (Luke 22:39–40), as well as where He set out on His entry to Jerusalem as King

21. From an "off air" discussion between Pope Paul and Patriarch Athenagoras, who were unaware that their microphones were still on. See Federico Serana, "An 'Off-Air' Extraordinary Story: The Secret Dialogue between Paul VI and Patriarch Athenagoras," *Notizie Italia News*, January 7, 2014, original source: www.incrocinews.it.

22. Of the members of these entourages, the sole surviving delegate is Metropolitan Evangelos of Perghe, then the young attending patriarchal deacon.

of Israel seated on a donkey (John 12:12–19), spent the night of His betrayal (Matt. 26:35–46), and later ascended to heaven (Acts 1:9–12). And it is on this mountain that tradition predicts the second coming of Christ will take place.

The two leaders held a private conference for ten minutes; once more, a few minutes of personal conversation broke a silence of centuries. After this, the Pope addressed the Patriarch in the presence of their respective entourages. The Patriarch offered a gold encolpion (pectoral medallion) and a special cross to the Pope, the latter being a souvenir from the recent millennial celebrations on Mount Athos in the summer of 1963. The meeting was sealed by the recital of the seventeenth chapter of St. John's Gospel by the two leaders as well as the repetition of the Lord's Prayer in Latin and Greek. Finally, the two prelates exchanged an embrace on the terrace and blessed the crowds that had gathered in the garden below. At 4 p.m., the Pope departed for Rome, while the Patriarch left for Bethlehem at 11 a.m. in order to concelebrate the Feast of the Nativity with Patriarch Benedictos of Jerusalem in the ancient basilica of Bethlehem according to the Julian calendar adhered to in the Holy Land.

In his address to the Pope, Patriarch Athenagoras noted:

It was in this holy land that the voice of the Lord was heard and treasured, proclaiming the gospel of reconciliation and salvation; only moments before His passion, he prayed with sweat for the preservation of His disciples in truth and unity. . . . Christianity has for centuries lived in the night of division. Its eyes are heavy in beholding the darkness. May this encounter of ours be the dawning of a bright and sacred day, when the coming Christian generations will share the same Cup. . . . Look how in embracing one another, together we encounter the Lord. Let us, therefore, continue the sacred way that opens before us. Then He will approach us and journey with us, as He once did with the two disciples on the road to Emmaus, indicating the way we should walk and rendering our steps swift toward our desired goal. (January 5, 1964)

In response on the following day, January 6, 1964, Pope Paul VI underlined the importance of "the Catholic Church and the Patriarchate of Constantinople, through their highest and holy representatives, meeting once again, after so many centuries of silence and hope." He recognized that this encounter was "one of [Pope John XXIII's] most beloved aspirations, which he constantly expressed in prayer to God until the end of his life." He also added, "The ways toward unity are long and permeated with many difficulties. Nevertheless, these roads incline toward each other and converge in the sources of the Gospel."

In their joint communiqué, the two Church leaders declared: "As two pilgrim-prelates, with our eyes fixed on Jesus Christ, the source of unity and peace, we pray that this encounter will prove to be a sign and foretaste of many similar occasions in the future, for the glory of God and the enlightenment of all humanity. After a silence of so many centuries, we have met here today with a mutual desire to fulfill the will of our Lord and promulgate the ancient truth of His Gospel entrusted to the Church" (January 6, 1964).

Archbishop Iakovos characterized the event as a "communion of love":

> The addresses of the two leaders, the warmth and candor of their words, their gestures and movements, their joint recitation of the Lord's Prayer, their reading in common of the seventeenth chapter of St. John's Gospel, and their shared blessing—from our Patriarchate as well as from Mount of Olives on the morning of January 6th—on the clergy and other faithful: all these bear witness to one thing alone, namely the *communion of love*, which is the necessary prerequisite for all other communion between the Churches. . . . Nothing else took place: neither formal discussions nor comprises or any such conventionalities. The communion of love is what prevails today between East and West after a lapse of many centuries. And my personal wish is that this communion may be further cultivated, acquire still more solid form, if possible, becoming the conscience and experience of our Churches so as to lead, on the day and hour ordained by the Lord, to the stability of the holy churches of God and the union of all, just as we Orthodox all pray unceasingly and sincerely.[23]

23. Constantelos, *Encyclicals and Documents of the Greek Orthodox Archdiocese of North and South America*, 790. My translation.

A Dialogue of Love Begins

Over the next ten days, the two prelates exchanged an additional four written communications, something inconceivable only six months earlier. Thus, the historical "dialogue of love"— a term coined by Metropolitan Meliton of Chalcedon— between Patriarch Athenagoras and Pope Paul VI established the basis for gradually and honestly breaking down barriers of centuries. This was followed a little less than two years later—in another joint declaration, which was read publicly at St. Peter's during the Second Vatican Council and in the Patriarchal Church at the Phanar—with the unprecedented "mutual lifting of the anathemas" on December 7, 1965,[24] when the same two prelates "removed from both the memory and the midst of the Church the sentences of excommunication" dating back to 1054.[25]

24. The expression of regret by the two prelates for actions on the part of their respective Churches that ultimately led to the formal excommunication and schism was observed in a joint declaration, which was a major event of the Second Vatican Council. Patriarch Athenagoras referred to the divisive excommunications as "a heavy and sinful burden." See his address to Pope Paul in St. Peter's Basilica during his visit to Rome on October 26, 1967.

25. What is often overlooked is that the excommunications in fact only affected the papal delegates under Cardinal Humbert on the one side and the Patriarch Michael Caerularius and his cohorts on the other side. Never were the two Churches sweepingly excommunicated. Nor, again, were the excommunications technically valid on the Roman Catholic side, since Pope Leo, who had commissioned the delegates, had died before the unfortunate actions occurred. Nonetheless, 1054 remains the date attributed to the schism between the two Churches. Of course, the "lifting of the anathemas" never implied restoration of full union between the two Churches—whether doctrinal, sacramental, or

In turn, this was followed within two years by the establishment of a paramount and hitherto uninterrupted tradition, namely the exchange of formal annual delegations at the respective Patronal Feasts of the two sister churches, which first commenced in 1969—in Rome on June 29 for the feast of Saints Peter and Paul and in Istanbul on November 30 for the feast of St. Andrew the Apostle. These momentous initiatives were the prelude to and culminated almost a decade later with the creation—during the papal visit to the Phanar on November 30, 1979—of the joint international commission for theological dialogue between the Roman Catholic Church and the Orthodox Church.[26] Thus, the Holy See and fourteen autocephalous Orthodox Churches commenced the official theological "dialogue of truth" on May 29, 1980, during the tenure of the late Ecumenical Patriarch Demetrios, and the successor to Pope Paul VI, the late Pope John Paul II. Thus

---

canonical—but it was an immense symbolical gesture of their remorse and goodwill for wrongdoings of the past. In his address to the Cardinals and members of the Bishops' Conference in Rome (October 26, 1967), Patriarch Athenagoras declared that "the time of reunion may well come slowly; but the time of love is the present." On the first anniversary of the lifting of the anathemas, Patriarch Athenagoras wrote to Paul VI: "This is the time for Christian courage. Let us love one another in order to confess our former common faith."

26. Pope John Paul was the first Bishop of Rome to pay a formal visit to the Ecumenical Patriarchate on the occasion of the latter's patronal feast on November 30, just one year after his papal election. Pope Benedict was elected in 2005 and was invited to visit the Church of Constantinople in 2006, while Pope Francis celebrated his inaugural Mass in 2013 and has been invited to visit the Ecumenical Patriarchate in November 2014.

began "a dialogue on an equal footing," the process for examining jointly, diligently, and openly the doctrinal differences between our two sister Churches.

One of the more spiritual and moving results of the more favorable relations between the two Churches has been the return of sacred relics, which originally were treasured in the East but were relocated to the West following the various crusades. Among these precious, albeit partial, relics relocated were those of St. Andrew to Patras (September 1964, by Pope Paul VI) and St. Titus to Crete (May 1966, by Pope Paul VI), as well as Saints Gregory the Theologian (December 2004, by Pope John Paul II) and John Chrysostom (December 2004, by Pope John Paul II) to Constantinople.

By way of conclusion, it is fitting to reiterate and underscore the words of Pope Paul VI and Ecumenical Patriarch Athenagoras upon their return to their respective sees. In a brief telegram to the Patriarch dated January 8, 1964, Pope Paul described the "unforgettable pilgrimage" that formed the context of their encounter and conveyed his "prayer that God may deem worthy to multiply it for the benefit of all Christianity."[27] In his brief response to the Pope, the Patriarch "addressed a fraternal greeting in the fellowship of love, wholeheartedly expressing his hope that the sacred voice that spoke so many good things to our hearts from the All-Holy Sepulcher may guide and strengthen the entire Christian world in the realization of God's holy will" (January 10, 1964).

27. Archives of the Chief Secretariat at the Phanar.

As for Pope Paul VI, he addressed the faithful gathered in St. Peter's Square to welcome him back to Rome on January 6, 1964: "You must appreciate that my trip was not just a unique spiritual event. It has proven to be an event of great historical significance. It is a link in the eternal chain of tradition. Who knows? It could also be the herald of new events of great and abundant benefit to the Church and humanity."

One year later, in a telegram to the Pope dated January 2, 1965, Patriarch Athenagoras "recall[ed] the first anniversary of that blessed encounter"; and, in remembrance of the Pope's remarks in French, bid him "au revoir."

May 2014: A Reaffirming Embrace

Relations between the two sister churches have improved so dramatically—despite setbacks in regional circumstances and tensions in theological dialogue—that communication and contact between regional and global leaders as well as even between local parishes and individual practitioners are today almost taken for granted. Nonetheless, the personal and spontaneous decision by His All-Holiness Ecumenical Patriarch Bartholomew to attend the inaugural Mass of the current Pope Francis in St. Peter's Square on March 19, 2013, sent commentators scurrying to the history books. The media inaccurately presented the event as completely unprecedented in the history of the two Churches since the schism that separated Eastern and Western Christendom in the eleventh century. However, the exchange of the kiss of peace, the liturgical symbol of unity among Christians, between Pope Francis and

Ecumenical Patriarch Bartholomew was an extraordinary expression of the goodwill between the two leaders for greater cooperation and fuller reconciliation.

Only three months later, in his address to Pope Francis during the formal visit of the Patriarchal Delegation to the Vatican led by His Eminence Metropolitan John of Pergamon—Orthodox cochair of the international theological commission for dialogue between the Roman Catholic and Orthodox Churches—on the occasion of the Patronal Feast of Saints Peter and Paul (June 29, 2013), Ecumenical Patriarch Bartholomew—himself once a protégé of the late Patriarch Athenagoras—underlined his commitment to the efforts toward unity:

Behold, with confident anticipation, we now contemplate our mutual journey to the common cup. We are not ignorant of the existing impediments to the desirable unity of all Christians. Nevertheless, we shall not cease working with all our strength and aspiring to the All-Holy Spirit. According to Gregory the Theologian, Archbishop of Constantinople, "this Spirit is most prudent and extremely loving; if it should discover fishermen, it can lure to Christ the entire world, captivating them by the fishing net of the word," just as Peter did. Indeed, "it can transform the passion of fanatical persecutors and create a Paul in the place of Saul, captivating them with the same intensity of piety as they had been captivated by evil. Such is the Spirit of meekness." Today, the same Spirit also renders us "bold heralds" of Christian unity, for whose sake we ceaselessly "bend our knees before the Father of our Lord Jesus Christ.

For this Spirit always was, is, and shall be; it is without beginning and without end." Thus it shall always inspire in us the desire for unity in simplicity and the salvation of all.

By way of affirmation and confirmation of this proposed journey, the Ecumenical Patriarch repeated the same invitation during the Thronal Feast of St. Andrew the Apostle on November 30, 2013, addressing the official delegation of Pope Francis to the Phanar led by Kurt Cardinal Koch, president of the Pontifical Council for Promoting Christian Unity and Roman Catholic cochair of the international theological commission for dialogue between the Roman Catholic and Orthodox Churches:

His Holiness brother Pope Francis and our Modesty have already exchanged ideas and opinions on these matters during our encounter in Rome. Indeed, as a first step of outreach toward the world, as an affirmation of our desire to increase our efforts toward Christian and peaceful reconciliation, we are planning a meeting in Jerusalem—to demonstrate our common will to advance along the path paved by our predecessors—in the new year that is upon us, which marks the fiftieth anniversary since the time when the two great contemporary church leaders, Patriarch Athenagoras and Pope Paul VI, met in the place where the sacred feet of our Lord once walked. In so doing, they carved a new historical path, which milestone we must honor in spirit and truth, surrendering the rest to the will of our Lord. As two ecclesiastical and spiritual leaders, we shall meet in order to address an appeal and invitation to all people, irrespective of faith and virtue, for a dialogue that ultimately aims at the knowledge of Christ's truth and the taste of the immense joy, which attends their acquaintance with Christ. However, this can ultimately only be achieved through the restoration of an inward separation from one another and through the unity of all people in Christ, which is truly the fullness of love and joy.

In an interview for Vatican Radio on January 18, 2014, Kurt Cardinal Koch described the upcoming meeting between Pope Francis and Ecumenical Patriarch Bartholomew as "the most important [ecumenical] opportunity for 2014" and expressed his hope that the meeting in Jerusalem "between the Ecumenical Patriarch Bartholomew and Pope Francis can be a new opportunity, with as much engagement and passion for unity as was present in 1964."[28]

At the entrance to St. Peter's Basilica in Rome, above the Sancta Porta, which the Pope opens only on jubilee celebrations, a marble inscription in Latin and Greek reads: "For the reconciliation of full communion between the Orthodox and Roman Catholic Churches, there was a meeting of prayer in this basilica between Pope Paul VI and Patriarch Athenagoras I on October 26, 1967, and between Pope John Paul II and Patriarch

---

28. See "Cardinal Koch on Christian Unity and Jewish-Catholic Relations," Vatican Radio, January 18, 2014, http://en.radiovaticana.va/news/2014/01/18/cardinal_koch_on_christian_unity_and_jewish-catholic_relations/en1-764917

Dimitrios I on December 6, 1987. To God alone is due honor and worship to the ages."

Athenagoras and Paul VI were great visionaries; their "great spirits could see into the future" (Wisdom of Sirach 48:24). Another important step toward "reconciliation of full communion" is the May 25, 2014, encounter between Pope Francis and Ecumenical Patriarch Bartholomew. May it be in accordance with God's will.

2

BREATHING WITH
BOTH LUNGS

Fifty Years of
the Dialogue of Love

∞∞∞∞∞∞∞∞∞∞∞

Brian E. Daley, S.J.

A number of years ago, when I was still teaching at the Weston
Jesuit School of Theology in Cambridge, Massachusetts, my
phone rang one winter afternoon, just as I was getting ready to
go home for the day. A young voice on the other end of the
line identified himself: "Father Daley? You don't know me,
but my name is Alex, and I wanted to ask you about the *Filioque*." It was getting late, and my heart sank a little as Alex
went on to explain why he was calling me: It seems that he
was the son of a Roman Catholic mother and a Greek Orthodox father, that he had been raised in each of the two Church
traditions for part of his life, and that he was then active in an
Orthodox parish somewhere in the Boston area. He said he
was struggling to discover for himself which Church was the
true Church of Christ and had asked a variety of people what
the real differences are that distinguish one tradition from the
other. His Orthodox priest had told him that any differences
are really summed up in the *Filioque*: the Western doctrine

that the Holy Spirit comes forth eternally, within the Mystery of God's being, not simply from the Father (as Jesus indicates in John 15:26), but also from the Son—a doctrine that the Roman Catholic Church eventually allowed to be added to the Latin translation of the creed of the ecumenical Council of Constantinople (381), although it does not belong to the Greek original of that document. Alex wanted to know the Catholic position on this, and why Catholics continued to confess the origin of the Holy Spirit in this way—as being "from the Father *and* the Son"—when they recited the creed; someone had given him my name as a person who was likely to know. So he had called to ask: Who's right?

Like any good academic, of course, I cleared my throat and began to bob and weave. This is really a complicated question, I told him; there are historical aspects to it as well as theological ones, and it involves looking not just at what Scripture says, but also at the development of theological language in the early Church. Then, too, I said, one had to remember that the long dispute between the Orthodox and Catholic Churches on the question really concerned not just the origin of the Spirit (about which, in any case, we can't say very much at all, since it is buried in the Mystery of God), but also Church structures and procedures, papal primacy and teaching authority, even the history of liturgical practice. I could recommend some books to him, I told him, or perhaps even meet once or twice to talk about some of these things in more detail. Then he interrupted me: "You don't understand, Father," he said. "I've already read a lot about this; I just want you to tell me, as a Catholic priest, whether the idea of the *Filioque* is *true* or not. And how do we know? And you've got to tell me quickly, because I'm calling from a pay phone, and I don't have another quarter!" As I spluttered helplessly, a recorded message from the phone company about time limits suddenly interrupted us, and our contact was broken.

Alex never called back (this was before cell phones), and I never learned how he had solved his problem; I hope he did, with the guidance of that Holy Spirit, who certainly is bestowed on each of us from the heart of God. But it has often seemed to me since that this little incident in some ways sums up much of Orthodox-Catholic relations over the past twelve centuries or so, since the Western Emperor Charlemagne's rivalry with Byzantium. That one Latin word, *Filioque*, has come to represent to many in both East and West the core of what they find deficient in the theology and Church structure of the other side of Christianity—in Vladimir Lossky's phrase, "the sole dogmatic grounds for the separation of East and West":[1] to the Orthodox, it savors of Western rationalism, papal authoritarianism, and "Christomonism"—the Western Christian tendency to emphasize the centrality of Christ at the expense of the more mysterious, less concretely imaginable role of the Holy Spirit, "which blows where it will" (John 3:8); to Catholics, it embodies the reluctance of Orthodoxy to accept doctrinal development

---

1. Vladimir Lossky, "The Procession of the Holy Spirit in Orthodox Trinitarian Doctrine," in *In the Image and Likeness of God* (Crestwood, N.Y.: St. Vladimir's, 1974), 71.

or liturgical adaptation, its fixation on early Greek formulations of doctrine, and its apparent disdain for the alternative traditions of the great theologians of the West. To both, it has remained a scandal, and a continuing justification for continuing to go our separate ways.

In October 2003, the North American Orthodox-Catholic Theological Consultation issued an agreed statement on the scriptural roots, the historical development, and the theological dimensions of this centuries-old debate, titled "The *Filioque*: A Church-Dividing Issue?" We did not, I think, reach the kind of clarity about the procession of the Holy Spirit that would have let us together give Alex a clear and simple answer, before his coin ran out; but we did feel we had studied the complex history of this question in the Scriptures and in the theological traditions of West and East enough to conclude "that our traditions' different ways of understanding the procession of the Holy Spirit need no longer divide us." What became clear to our Consultation, in fact, in the course of more than four years of common prayer and study, is that the origin of the Holy Spirit within the Mystery of God, as God and as a distinct, eternal hypostasis or person in relation to both Father and Son, is an aspect of the Christian faith that still requires further theological reflection, drawing on both our traditions; we even dared to suggest "that the time may now be at hand to return to this question together, in a genuinely ecumenical spirit, and to seek for new developments in our articulation of the apostolic faith that may ultimately win ecumenical Christian reception," perhaps at some new and genuinely ecumenical Council of the future.

Some History

This continuing, officially sponsored dialogue among American theologians of the Orthodox and Roman Catholic traditions—which has been at times, if only by default, the world's main forum for constructive Orthodox-Catholic conversation—reaches back almost fifty years, to the heady days during and after Vatican II. Dialogue and rapprochement were in the air. As one of the first journeys of his papacy, Pope Paul VI had made a pilgrimage to Jerusalem, early in January 1964, where he was warmly met by Ecumenical Patriarch Athenagoras, Archbishop of Constantinople–New Rome, and joined him in an embrace of love, and in a conversation full of ecumenical promise. Nine months later, on November 21, 1964, the Council's document on the Catholic Church and ecumenism, *Unitatis Redintegratio*, was finally approved, at the end of the third session. Proclaiming "the restoration of unity among all Christians" to be "one of the principal concerns of the Second Vatican Synod," the document labels the divisions among Churches and communities that have marked Christian life since its beginnings as "clearly contrary to Christ's will."[2] Acknowledging that all those who believe in Christ and are validly baptized "are in some kind of communion with the Catholic Church, even if that communion is not complete,"[3] the document recognized the considerable achievements of the worldwide ecumenical movement of the twentieth century, and urged all

2. *Unitatis Redintegratio*, 1.
3. Ibid., 3.

Catholic Christians to participate in ecumenical prayer and dialogue as part of the renewal and conversion of heart, within a new sense of the Church's identity and mission, to which all the Council's documents invited them.[4] Within this effort of rebuilding a visible, sacramentally realized unity in the whole Christian body, the document makes clear, collaboration and dialogue leading toward renewed communion with the Eastern Churches must take a privileged place, because of our common heritage of apostolic faith, priesthood, and sacraments.

The new Catholic attitude expressed at Vatican II invited new initiatives throughout the world, and they were not long in coming. At the beginning of March 1965, the Orthodox theologian Father Paul Schneirla (still active in our North American Consultation until a few years ago) wrote on behalf of the Standing Committee of Canonical Orthodox Bishops in the Americas to Baltimore's Cardinal Lawrence Shehan, the chair of the newly formed Catholic Bishops' Committee on Ecumenical Affairs, proposing the establishment of "a continuing theological dialogue" between Orthodox and Catholic theologians in the United States. The first meeting of the dialogue, characterized rather cautiously as "an informal discussion" in the brief press release devised for the occasion, was held at the parish hall of St. Spyridon's Greek Orthodox Church in Worcester, Massachusetts, on Thursday, September 9, 1965, under the joint chairmanship of Fr. Schneirla (representing Greek Orthodox Archbishop Iakovos) and Catholic Bishop Bernard Flanagan of Worcester, who was himself about to leave

4. Ibid., 4, 7–8.

for Rome and the Council's final session. The purpose of that first meeting of what was to become our Consultation, it seems, was mainly organizational: drawing up a long-range agenda and ironing out a structure and a style for future conversation. But it is clear from the records and correspondence dealing with that day that the meeting did not go easily. What some participants refer to as "complications," others as "an impasse," arose, because the appointed Catholic delegation included three Eastern-rite Catholic priests (two of them Jesuits from Fordham), as well as one Roman-rite priest with biritual faculties. Apparently because of their presence on the Catholic side, Archbishop Iakovos did not feel he could attend, citing the anxiety among members of the Orthodox clergy that Rome's new proclamation of ecumenical openness and respect for Eastern Christianity might, in fact, lead to hasty attempts at sacramental reunion, even to active proselytism by Catholics among Orthodox individuals and parishes, under the old model of "uniate Churches."

A good deal of behind-the-scenes negotiation seems to have taken place during the year that followed that first shaky meeting, apparently with success. The two groups of theologians, now calling themselves the Joint Roman Catholic-Orthodox Consultation, met a little more than a year later, on September 29, 1966, at the headquarters of the Greek Orthodox Archdiocese on Seventy-Ninth Street in New York. Archbishop Iakovos made it clear at the start of the meeting that it had the explicit encouragement and blessing of Patriarch Athenagoras, who, on December 7 of the previous year—three days after the closing session of Vatican II—had joined with Pope Paul VI in officially rescinding the mutual excommunications pronounced on each other by representatives of the Greek Orthodox and Roman Catholic communions in 1054. The conversation of this second North American meeting was again centered on defining the agenda and form of future sessions, but this time the atmosphere seems to have been one of hope, even excitement, rather than of caution. Fr. Alexander Schmemann, of St. Vladimir's Orthodox Seminary, remarked that this was probably the first occasion at which Roman Catholic and Orthodox theologians were engaging in officially sponsored, long-term discussion of central issues of faith since the first phase of the Council of Florence had ended in July 1439. Echoed by a number of participants on both sides, Fr. Schmemann went on to urge the group not to become just "another theological seminar for academic papers," but to apply itself to concrete questions of pastoral practice, as well as to the theoretical assumptions that underlie them. His colleague at St. Vladimir's, Fr. John Meyendorff, put this concern in a more lapidary style: "It should be agreed," he said, "that theology opposed to practice is bad theology, and that practice opposed to theology is bad practice. Furthermore," he added, "no valid theology avoids facing practical problems." These suggestions were apparently taken to heart; for the next meeting, scheduled for the following May, joint papers, each drafted by one Orthodox and one Catholic theologian, were to be prepared on theological diversity and unity within each tradition, on the practice of intercommunion, and on the Churches' common witness in modern theological education—conversation was to begin, in other words, with the consideration of concrete similarities and differences, and of the concrete ways in which each Church might grow more conscious of the other.

The Consultation was finally off and running—off and walking, at least! The policy suggested at the second meeting, of focusing first on the concrete issues of Christian life, rather than trying to solve the perennial questions that have held these two traditions apart, was generally followed for the first two decades of the Consultation's existence. The first joint statement of the Consultation, for instance, issued in December 1969, concerns the Eucharist, and is a little over a page in length: six terse theses expressing the fundamental points of agreement between the Orthodox and Catholic theological traditions on what the Eucharist is and does, while acknowledging the "serious differences . . . in our understanding of the Church, Eucharistic discipline and pastoral practice" that still prevent Eucharistic sharing. Other pastoral statements followed: on mixed marriages (1971) and on the sanctity of marriage (1978), on respect for life (1974) and the spiritual formation of children (1980), and on the situation in Eastern Europe as the Soviet empire was collapsing (1990), as well as brief sets of theses on the Church (1974), the pastoral office (1976), and the principle of *oikonomia*—the pastoral adaptation of theological and canonical rules (1976). A number of the documents issued by the Consultation during the 1980s and 1990s, too, were joint responses to the major statements of other ecumenical bodies: to the Faith and Order Commission's Lima Document, "Baptism, Eucharist and Ministry" (1984), for instance, and to the documents issued by the Joint International Commission for Catholic-Orthodox dialogue: "The Mystery of the Church and the Eucharist" (Munich, 1982), "Faith, Sacraments and the Unity of the Church" (Bari, 1987), the Sacrament of Order (New Valamo, 1988), and "Uniatism as a Means of Approaching Full Communion" (Balamand, 1993). In 1998, the Consultation issued a brief statement supporting the call by representatives of all the Christian Churches in the Arabic-speaking countries, meeting in Aleppo, to establish a common method for dating the Paschal celebration.

By the late 1980s, however, the Consultation seems to have felt it was ready—thanks to its increasingly happy experience as a group of committed Christian scholars listening to each other—to take on larger, more fundamental theological issues behind the centuries-old separation of our Churches, and to discuss them in greater fullness and depth. Acknowledging that Orthodox-Catholic differences always come down, in the end, to different conceptions of what the Church itself is and how it is authentically structured, the Consultation turned its attention in the late 1980s to issues of primacy and the synodal relationship of bishops: first in its 1986 statement "The Gift of Apostolicity in the Church," then in its related, but somewhat more substantial, 1989 statement "Conciliarity and Primacy in the Church." Discussion of the sensitive issue of the degree to which our two Churches recognize the validity of each other's baptisms, and therefore of their willingness not to rebaptize converts from the other tradition, eventually led to the Consultation's theologically rich and challenging 1999 statement, "Baptism and the Sacramental Economy." Meanwhile, the publication in September 1995 of a brief but suggestive new Vatican document reinterpreting the divisive issue of the procession of the Holy Spirit and the word *Filioque* in the Latin creed indicated a new openness on the part of the official Roman Catholic Church to recognize that the distinct approaches of Eastern and Western theology to this ancient and difficult question may not be mutually exclusive.[5] Inspired by this step, our North American Consultation began a series of discussions on the history and theology of the *Filioque* controversy in the fall of 1999, which led, after much detailed study, to what was surely its most substantial and perhaps our most theologically significant agreed statement until then: "The *Filioque*: A Church-Dividing Issue?," published in October 2003, mentioned above.

This statement is perhaps the most elaborate discussion of the *Filioque* as an ecumenical problem, from both the historical and the theological perspective, to be produced as a common project in modern times; yet it is, in the end, only a discussion, carefully crafted by a long-standing group of Orthodox and Catholic theologians, to advise and inform our bishops in North America. It is not, in itself, a resolution of this age-old source of pain and division; the Consultation's hope was that at least it would help create a new climate of understanding, a new context and a new stimulus for what Patriarch Athenagoras and Pope Paul VI, in their pioneering contacts of the 1960s and 1970s, so aptly christened "the dialogue of love" between our two Churches. But to move from this discussion, even from substantial agreement on the interpretation of our histories and from the analysis of our normative theological traditions

---

5. "The Greek and Latin Traditions Regarding the Procession of the Holy Spirit," *L'Osservatore Romano*, September 13, 1995.

that the statement attempts, to give birth to more concrete gestures of mutual acceptance, and ultimately to full sharing of the Eucharistic Mysteries, is something that lies beyond this Consultation's ability to act or decide, as theologians and pastors—a process for bishops and councils, whose resolution lies hidden in God's providential future.

Focusing Our Vision

Nevertheless, when we came to the end of that long process of drafting the statement on the *Filioque*, most members of the Consultation felt buoyed by the experience of finding an unexpectedly large expanse of common ground in the midst of one of ecumenism's most hard-fought battlefields; we had discovered anew that the willingness to read and reflect and listen together could lead, in the power of God's own Holy Spirit, to at least a deeper awareness of the context and origin of our differences, and to a greater willingness to move beyond them together toward new areas of concord. As a result, we felt ready to turn back to the neuralgic but inescapable question of the nature and role of primacy in the structures of the Church, especially papal primacy, and to explore the similarities and differences of our theological approaches to imagining and explaining ecclesial headship and its exercise of power, at its various levels. After several years of preliminary discussions, including a few false starts, we ended by producing a statement that was meant at least to characterize our present differences in understanding and realizing Church structure and authority, and to offer our own vision of what might be involved for both our Churches in moving beyond them. This vision is contained in the document "Steps Towards a Reunited Church: A Sketch of an Orthodox-Catholic Vision for the Future," which was published on October 2, 2010.

The statement begins by acknowledging that our different ways of understanding structure and authority in the Church remain the ultimate source of our divisions.

> It seems to be no exaggeration, in fact, to say that the root obstacle preventing the Orthodox and Catholic Churches from growing steadily towards sacramental and practical unity has been, and continues to be, the role that the bishop of Rome plays in the worldwide Catholic communion. While for Catholics, maintaining communion in faith and sacraments with the bishop of Rome is considered a necessary criterion for being considered Church in the full sense, for Orthodox, as well as for Protestants, it is precisely the pope's historic claims to authority in teaching and Church life that are most at variance with the image of the Church presented to us in the New Testament and in early Christian writings. In the carefully understated words of Pope John Paul II, "the Catholic Church's conviction that in the ministry of the bishop of Rome she has preserved, in fidelity to the Apostolic Tradition and the faith of the Fathers, the visible sign and guarantor of unity, constitutes a difficulty for most other Christians, whose memory is marked by certain painful recollections" (*Ut Unum Sint* 88). (2)

The document then sketches out briefly the historical developments in East and West that have led to these contrasting ecclesiologies: the Western sense of need for a central Church authority in the late Patristic and medieval world, as civil organization and cultural unity disintegrated around it; and the greater Eastern integration of Church life and teaching into the more unified public order of imperial Byzantine society.

Yet the statement asks whether the diverging ways we have each come to understand the Church's structure since the time of the early councils simply condemn us to permanent division. "It seems obvious to us," the authors continue, "that what we share, as Orthodox and Catholic Christians, significantly overshadows our differences" (4)—especially when we compare ourselves theologically and in practice to other Christian bodies. Both our Churches emphasize the continuity of apostolic teaching, as contained in Scripture and the creeds; the central, Church-constituting role of the Liturgy; and the foundational importance of baptism, chrismation, and the Eucharist in forming each Christian believer. Both tend to conceive of themselves today in what is called an "ecclesiology of communion," by which the Church itself is seen as represented most perfectly in the Eucharistic community presided over by a legitimately ordained bishop or one of his presbyters, who embody the continuity of apostolic authority and teaching. Both our Churches venerate Mary, the Mother of God; honor the Church's saints; value asceticism and various forms of the monastic life; and emphasize the importance of contemplative prayer as a way to holiness (4). In light of all that we share, and of the increasing social homogenization of modern society, it seems all the more tragic that we continue to see ourselves as spiritually and sacramentally alien to each other (5).

The statement goes on to paint in some of the details of what a possible structure of worldwide communion between our Churches might look like. It would have to be a form of what modern ecumenists often refer to as "reconciled diversity." Beginning with mutual recognition by the Orthodox and Catholic Churches as authentic embodiments of the Church of Christ, the "different parts of this single Body of Christ, drawing on their different cultural and spiritual traditions, would live in full ecclesial communion with each other without requiring any of the parts to forego its own traditions and practices" (6c). They would express this communion in liturgical sharing, concelebration, and mutual commemoration in prayer; regional and superregional synods would be convened regularly to deal with common theological and pastoral issues; and the Churches would attempt to realize together their mission to communicate the Gospel of Christ to the contemporary world (6f). In all of this, the continuing role of the bishop of Rome, which has for so long been a cause of disunion, would have to be carefully defined and realized, "both in continuity with the ancient structural principles of Christianity and in response to the need for a unified message in the world of today" (7). He would be regarded as the "first of the world's bishops and regional patriarchs," yet—in accord with the teaching of both Vatican Councils—"would be understood by all as having authority only within a synodal/collegial context: as member as well as head of the college of bishops" (7b). Echoing Pope John Paul II's encyclical *Ut Unum Sint*, the document continues, "The fundamental worldwide ministry of the bishop of Rome would be to promote the communion of all the local Churches: to call on them to remain anchored in the unity of the Apostolic faith, and to observe the Church's traditional canons. He would do this as a witness to the faith of Peter and Paul, a role inherited from his early predecessors who presided over the Church in that city where Peter and Paul gave their final witness" (7c).

The document then lists several major theological and canonical questions that the Consultation saw as needing to be resolved before this kind of reconciled diversity can be reached in an effective way; but it emphasizes again—quoting Cyril of Alexandria—how central a Eucharistically unified community of disciples is to the final vision of Christ. Cyril writes, "By liturgically blessing (*eulogōn*) those who believe in him into a single body—namely, his own—through sacramental participation, [Christ] has made them completely one body with himself and with each other. Who, after all, could divide, or alienate from natural unity with one another, those who are bound through the one holy body into unity with Christ? For if 'all of us partake of the one loaf' (1 Cor 10.17), all of us are formed into one body. It is impossible to divide Christ" (Commentary on John 11:11; see Steps 10). So the document itself concludes:

> The challenge and the invitation to Orthodox and Catholic Christians, who understand themselves to be members of Christ's Body precisely by sharing in the Eucharistic

gifts and participating in the transforming life of the Holy Spirit, is now to see Christ authentically present in each other, and to find in those structures of leadership that have shaped our communities through the centuries a force to move us beyond disunity, mistrust, and competition, and towards that oneness in his Body, that obedience to his Spirit, that will reveal us as his disciples before the world.

What Do Ecumenical Statements Achieve?

The fascination, as well as the dangers, of the kind of ecumenical enterprise undertaken in statements like those of the North American Consultation seem obvious. Ecumenical theological dialogue, after all, is a uniquely demanding, as well as a uniquely consoling form of religious conversation. To be successful at it—to engage in dialogue that is not only congenial but fruitful for those involved—requires time, expertise, and learning on the part of its participants, a commitment to doing the necessary homework in preparation for each meeting, a great deal of patience and self-control when tempers grow frayed or the conversation repetitious, and of course a sense of humor. It requires from each participant a clear commitment to his or her own theological and liturgical tradition, and the ability to articulate it honestly and completely, in a way that someone not from that tradition can understand; but it also requires a more than ordinary love for the traditions of the other side, a sympathetic understanding of their spirituality and liturgy, a desire to be nourished by their sources as much as by one's own. More practically, ecumenical dialogue usually builds on personal relationships, on shared backgrounds, on the ability of members to speak the same language culturally as well as verbally; surely one reason our North American Consultation has continued to work seriously and productively—even in the years between 2000 and 2007, when the international Orthodox-Catholic dialogue had, for all practical purposes, come to an ungracious halt—is our common set of assumptions, as Americans and Canadians, about what constitutes civil conversation, as well as the fact that many of us have been meeting together regularly for more than a quarter century, and deeply cherish each other's friendship. We like and trust each other.

Most important, perhaps, ecumenical dialogue really depends on the desire of everyone involved to move our Churches beyond the status quo, in which all of us, consciously or not, have a vested interest: It depends on the desire that there really should be, in some way we can now only vaguely imagine, a single communion of Orthodox and Catholic Christians that would allow our Churches to remain what we are, in everything that is truly of God, while proclaiming together a single faith, sharing (at least on extraordinary occasions) a single altar and a single cup, and recognizing in each other's bishops a single, if diversely articulated, prophetic structure, founded on a single apostolic tradition. We have to want this seriously enough to run the risk of change, and even of loss, in all that is not a part of the essence of Christian faith and life. And the real question that stands before our Churches is not whether they are ready to talk intelligently about unity, but whether they really desire that unity enough to let our dialogue change us in profound yet unforeseen ways. Such a desire, I suspect, must spring from more than normal human interests and motives, and can only become real and effective by the transforming, inner gift of the Holy Spirit. We wait on that gift.

As ecumenical dialogue between Catholic theologians and representatives of other Churches continues, it is becoming increasingly clear that on almost every issue that divides Christians—the Catholic Marian doctrines, the Eucharist, the role of the saints, or for Catholics and Orthodox the *Filioque*—the underlying, more fundamental issue is always that of Church structure and authority; more particularly, it is the role of the Pope as authoritative spokesman for the apostolic tradition of faith and effective center of the Church as a communion of communions, a Catholic Church of Catholic Churches. In his encyclical on Christian unity, *Ut Unum Sint*, mentioned above, Pope John Paul acknowledged his "particular responsibility . . . to find a way of exercising the primacy which, while in no way renouncing what is essential to its mission, is nonetheless open to a new situation." He continues:

> This is an immense task, which we cannot refuse and which I cannot carry out by myself. Could not the real but imperfect communion existing between us persuade Church leaders and their theologians to engage with me in a patient and fraternal dialogue on this subject, a dialogue in which, leaving useless controversies behind, we could listen to one

another, keeping before us only the will of Christ for his Church and allowing ourselves to be deeply moved by his plea "that they may all be one . . . so that the world may believe that you have sent me" (John 17.21)? (95–96)

Both our divisions and our road toward reunion, the late Pope seems to be saying, depend most centrally on the way we imagine and exercise Church authority. The real question facing Orthodox and Catholic Christians, I think, as we seek the way toward the full communion that can be expressed and nourished in Eucharistic sharing, is whether those ultimately in authority in our Churches—those who stand to lose the most in any process of institutional change—are ready to look beyond the traditions that have formed their present offices and to envision some new form of Church unity that is neither a centralized, bureaucratic institution nor a loose, charismatic confederation, that allows for local diversity of worship and spirituality and pastoral leadership while preserving structures for coming to real agreement on the essentials of the Church's faith and sacramental life. For the first ten centuries of Christianity, this kind of communion worked (most of the time); the challenge to us now is to discover a way—in the vastly different world of rock music and Coca-Cola and the Internet, where both homogeneity and local identity are highly charged issues—to let it become a reality again. But that will mean that both Churches, while remaining true to the core of their tradition of faith and worship, must become different from what they now are.

There is risk, then, in any sincere ecumenical dialogue: the risk facing both parties that an open exploration of Christian unity and Christian difference will call on us to change things that we cherish, in the life and the expression of faith of our Churches. In the same encyclical I have just quoted, *Ut Unum Sint*, Pope John Paul stresses the importance of dialogue in all human relations, whether individual or communal: "The capacity for dialogue is rooted in the nature of the person and his dignity," he writes, and is "an indispensable step along the path toward human self-realization" (28). But since dialogue always involves an opening of myself—my mind, my heart, my desires—toward another, a listening to the other and a reconsideration of our own most deeply rooted convictions in trusting company with the other, dialogue always must lead to what he calls an "examination of conscience" and a readiness for conversion. Quoting I John 1:10 ("If we say that we have not sinned, we make [God] a liar and his word is not in us"), the Pope continues:

Such a radical exhortation to acknowledge our condition as sinners ought also to mark the spirit, which we bring to ecumenical dialogue. . . . All the sins of the world were gathered up in the saving sacrifice of Christ, including the sins committed against the Church's unity: the sins of Christians, those of the pastors no less than those of the lay faithful. Even after the many sins, which have contributed to our historical divisions, Christian unity is possible, provided that we are humbly conscious of having sinned against unity and are convinced of our need for conversion. (34)

Only if ecumenical dialogue is ready to become a "dialogue of conversion," he suggests—borrowing a phrase from his predecessor, Paul VI—can it become an authentic "dialogue of salvation" (35).

The Groupe des Dombes, a study group of French Catholic and Protestant theologians that has gathered for ecumenical dialogue each year since 1937, has argued that such openness to repentance and conversion must, in fact, be an essential part of the life of Christian communities as well as Christian individuals, if the Church is truly to become what it claims to be in its creed: one, holy, catholic, and apostolic. In a 1993 statement, the group argues, "Ecclesial conversion is a constituent element of ecclesial identity. When fully and universally achieved, each confessional group will be the Church in full recognition of the ecclesial character of the others. There will no longer be partial, incomplete ecclesiality for any, either in its own environment or in that of the others. In particular that means the achievement and recognition of the identity of the Church's 'structure' in all the confessions. This therefore presupposes general doctrinal agreement on the 'structure' of the church."[6]

Idealistic as it sounds, the document is suggesting that the relentless search for such a common structure of Christian unity—one that does not suppress the identity of any of the

---

6. Groupe des Dombes, *For the Conversion of the Churches* (Geneva: WCC, 1993), 27.

Pope Paul VI and Ecumenical Patriarch Athenagoras (Courtesy of Aristeides Panotis)

Pope John Paul II and Ecumenical Patriarch Demetrios (Courtesy of *L'Osservatore Romano*)

Ecumenical Patriarch Bartholomew and Pope John Paul II (Courtesy of Nikolaos Manginas)

Pope Benedict XVI and Ecumenical Patriarch Bartholomew (Courtesy of Nikolaos Manginas)

Icon of Saints Paul (*left*), Andrew (*center*), and Peter (*right*). (Monastery of St. Catherine, Mt. Sinai, twelfth century)

Ecumenical Patriarch Bartholomew and Pope Francis (Courtesy of *L'Osservatore Romano*)

Churches, but that draws all of them together in charity, faith, and mutual recognition—is intrinsically linked to the change of heart, the *metanoia*, which is an indispensable part of all Christian life.

Ecumenical dialogue constantly confronts us with the nagging question of whether we are ready, even in principle, for such a conversion: ready to let go of our ecclesial individuality, our distinctness, our prized language and practices, as what St. Paul, in his Letter to the Philippians, calls *harpagmos*, "something to be grasped," and to "empty ourselves" as Christ did in becoming human, in order to take on together the "form of a servant" that will let us bring life to the world (see Phil. 2.5–11). For both the Orthodox and the Catholic Churches, the conversion that unity requires will surely involve a kind of ecclesial martyrdom: *martyria* in the sense of the witness that Jesus, in John 17:23, proposes as the real message of his disciples' unity, "that the world may know you have sent me"; but *martyria* also in the sense of laying down something that is part of our life, for the sake of our friends. For the Catholic Church, growth toward ecumenical unity must unquestionably involve the readiness to accept new forms of synodal decision making and teaching that will be more complex, more mutual, more inclusive, and less centralized than is conceivable within the classical modern model of papal primacy; for the Orthodox Churches, it will involve the development of new, open, and permanent structures for reaching binding consensus on the essentials of the Christian life, along with other Christians, and for witnessing to that life on a genuinely universal scale, even outside of those cultures where Orthodoxy has traditionally flourished.

For both the Catholic and the Orthodox Churches, our experience here in the pluralist, democratic setting of North America may prove to be a substantial help toward conceiving and realizing these new structures and procedures of communion. Hence the special promise, and the special responsibility, of Orthodox-Catholic dialogue in this culture for seeking out new possibilities and new frontiers. As Pope John Paul reminded us on more than one occasion, it is only when Orthodox and Catholic Christians think and act and pray together, aware of the fullness of both traditions, that the Body of Christ will begin again to "breathe with both its lungs."

In 1954, the French Dominican Yves Congar published a long, magisterial essay on the history and causes of the schism between Eastern and Western Christianity, as part of a massive, two-volume collection of studies honoring the great Belgian ecumenist Dom Lambert Beauduin (who had just turned eighty himself), and commemorating the ninth centenary of the mutual excommunications of 1054, usually regarded as the formal beginning of East-West schism.[7] Congar's essay was published in an expanded English version in 1959, several months after Pope John XXIII surprised the world by convoking an

---

7. *1054–1954: L'Église et les Églises: Neuf siècles de douloureuse séparation entre l'Orient et l'Occident*, Collection Irénikon (Chevetogne, 1954–55). Congar's essay, "Neuf cents ans après: Notes sur le 'Schisme oriental,'" is the opening essay of the collection: 1.3–95. The expanded English edition of the essay, with added material in both text and references, is Yves Congar, *After Nine Hundred Years* (New York: Fordham University Press, 1959).

Ecumenical Council, with the express purpose of opening new
doors toward Christian unity.

Congar's thesis, in this classic essay of sixty years ago, is
that the mutual "estrangement" (and he deliberately uses the
English word, even in his French original) between Eastern and
Western Christianity has deep roots in the religious culture of
both worlds that developed over centuries, beginning long
before 1054, and that led to growing prejudice and misun-
derstanding on both sides; it was this estrangement, he argues,
that caused both sides to accept the mutual condemnations of
1054 as final, despite repeated efforts by individual bishops
and theologians over the following centuries to resolve the
canonical and dogmatic issues behind that rupture. "Not that
the schism is of itself the estrangement," Congar adds; "rather,
the schism is the acceptance of the estrangement."[8] He goes
on to point to the theological and spiritual roots of schism,
which he suggests lie for both sides in an overly narrow, overly
self-referential conception of the reality of the Church—one
that fails to see in each local Eucharistic community a sacramental realization of the "one, holy, catholic and apostolic
Church" that by its very identity points toward real universal
communion:

> The sin of schism is already committed in the heart when
> we behave as though we were not an integral part of the
> whole with others, *alter alterius membra* (Rom 12.5). In this

8. Congar, *After Nine Hundred Years*, 89.

organic whole which is the Church, each local church not only realizes the mystical nature of the whole, mainly through the sacramental life, but is itself also *a part* of that whole, according to the plan of God which is to assemble all mankind into one Church and to represent, in the catholicity of that Church, the infinite riches of his gifts. . . . To accept each other really means that each one accepts the other as members of the same body, according to the vocation and function that is assigned to each part.[9]

Congar argues powerfully that this mutual acceptance, which alone can overcome our centuries of estrangement, is both a theological and a spiritual process, a conversion that involves, on both sides, the heart as well as the mind:

On the part of the East, there is need of an open-mindedness towards what is irreversible in the development of the theological theory of the Church [in the West], and in the fact of the primacy: not necessarily the primacy in all the modalities it has been made to take on by history, or even in its present-day form, for a great portion of these elements are of [a] relative and historical order; but a papacy in that minimal form compatible with a local ecclesiastical autonomy. . . .

On the part of the West and Rome, it all comes back to their accepting *in truth* the existence of an East, with its own mentality, its genius, its temperament, and its history,

9. Ibid., 89–90.

and the right it has to be known, accepted and loved for what it is.[10]

What almost fifty years of our North American dialogue have accomplished for both sides, I believe, has been to focus and foster understanding and desire on this long process of conversion: our understanding of the astounding richness and complexity of the traditions in which both sides have lived out their faith in Christ the Lord, and our desire to share those traditions fully, as our common Christian inheritance. In 2014, the present heads of our worldwide communions—Ecumenical Patriarch Bartholomew and Pope Francis—commemorate that historic embrace of fifty years ago, which began what Patriarch Athenagoras named "the dialogue of love" after over 900 years of hostility and silence, by meeting again in Jerusalem as brothers, to continue the conversation. Our desire to share, with them, in a new unity in faith and love is as strong today as it was then; but while much progress has been made in our growth toward honest understanding in these fifty years, we still look for the movement of God's Holy Spirit to guide our Churches toward a fuller, more concrete unity of life. We pray that such unity will be ours—in the way and at the time that God wills, with the surprising effects that only God can foresee.

In the meantime, all of us who have taken part in some kind of ecumenical dialogue are grateful for what these fifty years since 1964 have brought us, deepening in the leaders and

10. Ibid., 86–87, translation slightly altered.

faithful of both our Churches a prophetic spirit of understanding, relentlessly yearning, often frustrated ecumenical love. Now, near the end of our fifth decade of organized conversation (and still talking), we can only pray with St. Paul "that our love may abound more and more, with knowledge and all discernment, so that we may approve what is excellent, and may be pure and blameless for the day of Christ" (Phil. 1:10). We owe this to our Churches, and to our world.

3

"A SIGN OF CONTRADICTION"

A Reflection on the Meeting of the Pope and the Patriarch

✕✕✕✕✕✕✕✕✕✕✕✕

Georges Florovsky

Introduction by Matthew Baker

Father Georges Florovsky (1893–1979) spent his entire service of over five decades as an Orthodox theologian intensely involved in ecumenical dialogue at all levels. His thought and example continue to command respect from all corners of the Orthodox spectrum of opinion, from devoted career ecumenists to resolute critics of ecumenism and everything in between. A model and mentor to several generations of Orthodox theologians of diverse perspectives (V. Lossky, B. Krivocheine, A. Schmemann, J. Romanides, J. Meyendorff, Staretz Sophrony, and J. Zizioulas), "Father Georges Florovsky"—to quote the words of the recently canonized Serbian theologian and confessor Justin Popovich—"is already an icon on the *deisis* of Orthodox theology." It was Florovsky who in large part articulated the principles that have guided faithful Orthodox theologians engaging in ecumenical conversation to this day.

As a priest of the Ecumenical Patriarchate throughout his long theological career, Florovsky was present at the Pan-Orthodox meeting in Rhodes in the summer of 1959 and took part in the discussions there regarding prospects for an official Orthodox–Roman Catholic dialogue. Florovsky strongly supported a bilateral international theological dialogue between Orthodox and Roman Catholic theologians, and was also positive about Roman Catholic involvement in Faith and Order. Archival materials reveal, however, that he disagreed with the initial intention expressed in 1959 by Patriarch Athenagoras, Archbishop Iakovos Koukouzis, and WCC Secretary General Wilhelm Visser't Hooft to include within this Roman Catholic–Orthodox dialogue the various Protestant confessions. Although Florovsky did not live long enough to see the theological dialogue with Rome come to fruition, it is noteworthy that it was ultimately his vision in this matter that came to prevail.

Florovsky devoted surprisingly little detailed attention in his published work to the topic of Orthodox and Roman Catholic doctrinal differences. A thorough study makes clear, however, that in his mind the crucial issue was the papacy—an item he considered not unrelated to central matters of Christology and its import for the doctrine of the Church.[1] On the one hand, Florovsky was of the opinion that, historically

---

1. In sharp contrast to the polemics associated especially with V. Lossky, Florovsky gave little emphasis to differences regarding Trinitarian theology and the *Filioque,* and regarded this as an area where a yet unachieved synthesis was still possible. For his views on this matter, see the sources cited in the articles below at footnote 2 as well as the following: Matthew Baker, "The Eternal 'Spirit

speaking, medieval papal claims were largely responsible for the schism, and the later teaching of Vatican I reflected a false doctrine regarding the unity of the Church; on the other, he noted that neither side was without fault, and he insisted to his Protestant colleagues in the WCC that no true ecumenical unity could be conceived without including Rome and her ancient foundations. Florovsky was consistent throughout many decades of writing in recognizing sacramental grace and Eucharistic life within the Roman Catholic Church, insisting that the rigorist theory of *oikonomia* regarding reception of converts held by some Orthodox theologians was nothing more than a late-developed theological opinion—not the teaching of the Church. With this perspective, he called upon Orthodox theologians to appropriate within their own ecclesiological synthesis the sacramental theology of St. Augustine regarding charismatic life beyond the canonical boundaries of the Church. Florovsky's own ecclesiology, drawing especially from the patristic witness of Sts. Augustine, John Chrysostom, and Nicholas Cabasilas as well as later Russian sources, was likewise deeply informed by his reading of such Roman Catholic *ressourcement* figures as Émile Mersch, Dom Odo Casel, Karl Adam, Yves Congar, and Henri De Lubac. Florovsky demonstrated considerable open mindedness regarding possible future clarifications and adjustments in Roman Catholic theology regarding the doctrine of primacy, and expressed interest and hope in the

---

of the Son': Barth, Florovsky and Torrance on the Filioque," *International Journal of Systematic Theology* 12, no. 4 (October 2010): 382–403.

theological developments of the Second Vatican Council, in particular regarding its teaching on episcopal collegiality and the local Church, in which he detected signs of a return to ancient tradition.

Florovsky warned against the "sin" of hastiness in ecumenical relations, stressing the virtue of "ecumenical patience." He was a sharp critic of doctrinal minimalism and political pragmatism in ecumenical dialogue. Yet contrary to unsubstantiated claims made by certain interested parties since his death, a thorough study of his published corpus, interviews, and archives shows that Florovsky remained staunchly committed to ecumenism—as a Christian imperative—to the end, expressing no regret for the years of energy he had expended in this direction, even as it had diverted him from countless other unfinished theological projects. As he put it, ecumenical meeting had brought about a greater seriousness regarding theology.

According to Florovsky, a genuine meeting of the Orthodox with Rome would require a real clarification and theological development on the part of the Orthodox as regards their own ecclesiology. Significant signs of such clarification and development can now be seen taking place in the contemporary Orthodox-Catholic international dialogue, due not least to the salutary insights and leadership of Florovsky's student, Metropolitan John (Zizioulas) of Pergamon, whose immense achievements in the understanding of apostolic succession, synodality, and primacy now point the way forward for Orthodox theology and ecumenical dialogue. Here Florovsky's envisioned program of neopatristic synthesis—always an inherently ecumenical agenda—continues to show its renewed fecundity and promise, most especially as it converges with Roman Catholic theology's continued assimilation of its own twentieth-century patristic *ressourcement*.[2]

The present text of Florovsky that follows, written following the occasion of the 1964 Jerusalem meeting between Patriarch Athenagoras and Pope Paul VI, was originally published in Russian as "Знамение Пререкаемо" in the Paris journal *Вестник Русского Студенческого Христианского Движения* (nos. 72–73, I–II, 1964, 1–7. Until recently, it remained entirely unnoticed, and it was not cited in the existing scholarship on Florovsky or on the ecumenical dialogue.[3] We offer the text now both for its historical interest and in the conviction that Father Georges's sage and balanced counsel still remains relevant and worthy of consideration today—even under the

2. For a detailed study of the inherently ecumenical design of Florovsky's conception of neopatristic synthesis as well as its varied development in Lossky and Zizioulas, see Matthew Baker, "Neopatristic Synthesis and Ecumenism: Toward the 'Reintegration' of Christian Tradition," in *Eastern Orthodox Encounters of Identity and Otherness: Values, Self-Reflection, Dialogue*, ed. Andrii Krawchuk and Thomas Bremer (New York: Palgrave-Macmillan, 2014), 235–260. For a succinct overview of Florovsky's ecumenical thinking and activities, see Matthew Baker and Seraphim Danckaert, "Georges Florovsky," in *Orthodoxy and Ecumenism: A Handbook for Theological Education*, ed. Pantelis Kalaitzidis, Thomas FitzGerald, Cyril Hovorun, Aikaterini Pekridou, and Nikolaos Asproulis (Geneva: World Council of Churches, Conference of European Churches, and the Volos Academy for Theological Studies, forthcoming).

3. For a thorough bibliography of the scholarly literature on Florovsky in multiple languages, see Matthew Baker, "Bibliography of Literature on the Life and Work of Father Georges V. Florovsky," *Записки русской академической группы в США/Transactions of the Association of Russian-American Scholars in the U.S.A.* 37 (2011–12): 473–547.

changed conditions of a theological dialogue now long since commenced and progressing fruitfully in the decades since Florovsky's death. Thanks are offered to Dr. Alexis Klimoff (Vassar College, N.Y.) for help with the present translation and to the Rev. Dr. John Chryssavgis for his encouragement and invitation to publish this text here.

<><><><><><><><><><>

"A Sign of Contradiction"[4]

> He calleth to me out of Seir, Watchman, what of the night?
> Watchman, what of the night? The watchman said, The
> morning cometh, but it is still night. (Isaiah 22:11)

The meeting of two patriarchs—of the new and the old Rome, long separated from each other—was unquestionably a significant event. And the venue, chosen deliberately—the Holy Land, the land of great fulfilled promises, the land of sacred memories, the land of Christ Himself—gave to the event an

---

4. The title of the original Russian, "Знамение Пререкаемо," is drawn from the Slavonic version of Luke 2:34 (cf. also Acts 28:22). The original sense is that of a "sign [that is] spoken against," or "a sign which shall be spoken against" (King James Version). The shorthand of "a sign of contradiction" is based on the Douay-Rheims translation, "for a sign which shall be contradicted," which in turn reflects the Vulgate text of the same verse: *in signum cui contradicetur*. We have opted for this translation for its literary succinctness as well as its currency and ready recognition within the English-speaking Catholic world, thanks to its use by Pope John Paul II, who spoke of this phrase as giving "a distinctive definition of Christ and of his Church": see Karol Wojtyla, *Sign of Contradiction* (New York: Seabury, 1979), 8.

especially solemn, even symbolic, character. Indeed, some perceived it as a miracle.

The importance of the event is quite obvious. But it is much more difficult to unravel its full meaning and to determine its value. In any case, the meeting of the patriarchs was an unexpected event, almost a surprise. Few were prepared for it inwardly, in psychological and spiritual terms, even among those who were ready to welcome it sincerely. It therefore immediately gave birth to rumors and incomprehension. Some embraced it with joy as a favorable sign. For others it was deeply troubling. Among many Orthodox this meeting even caused alarm and suspicion, generating wariness, passion, and fear. This could and should have been expected, and to remain silent about it now it would be foolhardy. Rome as a topic is a painful one for the Orthodox. All too many troubling memories, disappointments, and bitter experiences are connected with it. It is difficult to disregard these memories, nor would it be appropriate to disregard them. Sober historical memory is the indispensable guarantee of responsible action. But memory must not shackle movement. One cannot act based solely on historical precedent. History is not locked into repeating itself—it is an ongoing creative process. What was impossible yesterday might become possible tomorrow. Conditions change; new people replace the old. New perspectives may appear, opening new possibilities.

From the Orthodox point of view, the topic of Rome is the principal and basic ecumenical question. It is the starting point of "Christian division," the tip and the root of the "schism." In a certain sense we are right to speak of the "undivided" Church

61

of the first Christian millennium, even though there was division then as well. The idea of "One Church" was however a firm component of the Christian consciousness of the time. The "division of the Churches"—if this injudicious and ambiguous expression should be used at all—begins precisely with the break between Byzantium and Rome. The unity of the Christian world was shattered at that very point. Seen in the universal perspective, this was the central catastrophe or tragedy of Christian history. The history of this break has been described many times, and from different points of view. A completely impartial account of this sad history is difficult to achieve. In great part it was the result of misunderstandings, a consequence of human frailty, stubbornness, and sin. The division could probably have been avoided. In fact, for a long time many refused to accept its reality. History is made up of human decisions. It depends on human freedom, sometimes clear-eyed and insightful, but often quite blind. Of course events could have proceeded differently. However we now face the reality of an effected separation, and referring to unrealized possibilities does not solve our current problem. Is it possible to restore the lost unity, and should we even strive to achieve this goal? Or, alternatively, should we be reconciled to the separation as final and irreversible, and consider any attempt to "reunite" as hopeless and rather dangerous? It would seem that historical experience suggests the most pessimistic answer to this question. In fact, the "division" was reinforced above all by clumsy and hasty attempts at "reunion," and the memory of these episodes weighs heavily on the mind and heart of the Orthodox. In the final analysis, does this mean that one must give up all hope and be locked into disunity? Must one reject any glimmer of hope with distrust and suspicion?

Some years ago (in 1950), Professor Ioannis Karmiris spoke at the University of Athens on the occasion of the celebration of the Three Saints[5] on this very subject: the schism of the Roman Church. His speech was devoted to the history of the separation. He concluded by raising the question whether reunion was a possibility. Despite all the sad lessons of history, he emphasized, a peaceful resolution of the disagreements between the Orthodox Church and the Roman Church nevertheless remains possible—given the right conditions, "by means of oikonomia." The separation should not be considered final and unsurmountable. On the contrary, it must be overcome and can be overcome. Only this will require, above all, a long and serious preparation of the hearts and minds of both Churches, of the clergy as well as the laity. Prof. Karmiris was convinced that the Orthodox Church must not shy away from collaboration with Rome in this enterprise, and that it must hope to resolve existing differences to "by means of oikonomia," restoring harmony, love, and unity between the two churches.

This judgment of a theologian and historian as careful and discreet as Professor Karmiris calls for serious consideration. It is not entirely clear what he means by the phrase of "by way of oikonomia." But in any case it is clear that he does not think that "reunification" can take place without a substantial agreement, without resolving controversial issues. It was his belief

---

5. The feast of the Three Holy Hierarchs, celebrated in the Orthodox Church on January 30.

that these issues could be resolved, given the goodwill of both parties. In effect, he invites both Churches to a responsible *theological dialogue*—based on the Word of God and the ancient Tradition of the Church, and conducted in a spirit of mutual respect and love. One must not expect such a dialogue to be easy and lead to quick resolution of all differences and doubts. On the contrary, one must anticipate that it will be lengthy and difficult, if only it can manage to be honest and deep. But this is not a sufficient reason to refrain from dialogue, or to avoid it. The main obstacle to ecumenical progress has always been ecumenical impatience and ecumenical hastiness. This always leads toward a simplification of problems. The past history of relations between Orthodoxy and Rome demonstrates the danger of such haste, and its futility. But it seems that under present conditions the dialogue may prove to be easier than even a few years ago. The Roman Church is now in the process of reviewing her theological traditions, and in many ways is returning to the Tradition of the Ancient Church. This creates conditions favorable for dialogue.

A dialogue is primarily a meeting. In many circles—both in Rome and among the Orthodox—there is now a real will to meet. Meeting has already occurred at a distance—in the theological literature. We must first of all get to know one another. The problem of mutual familiarization must be tackled at all levels. Most fruitful of all would be joint study and discussion of the main themes of the Christian faith, based on the Word of God and in the context of the Tradition of the Church. This would be the beginning of the "preparation of hearts and minds" mentioned by Professor Karmiris. The problem of separation must be posed with complete honesty. And this will inevitably lead to the discovery that the very meaning and nature of "division" is understood differently in Rome and in the Orthodox Church. It follows that the question of "reunification" is also seen differently. This does not mean however that the first task of the dialogue must necessarily be the topic of "reunification" as such. This topic will arise of itself in the process of dialogue. To begin with it would be premature. It is necessary first of all to reach the conviction that "reunification" is a real task and not an artificial one, that the very being, the very nature of the Church requires it. The phrase, which is now so often abused—*separated brothers*—will be filled with living meaning only when it is experienced as an acute pain of separation, sorrow over separation, when the depth and reality of the schism are clearly realized.

The method of theological dialogue can only be *ecumenism in time*.[6] A true meeting of the divided East and West is possible only within the element of Church Tradition. The futility of the method of "comparative theology" has long been apparent in the experience of the ecumenical movement, and has already been abandoned. We must return to the sources. However, "ecumenism in time" does not mean a *retreat to antiquity*, nor does it mean a simple *return to the past*. Tradition

---

6. In a letter dated October 21, 1973, to the Scottish Reformed theologian Thomas F. Torrance, Florovsky noted that he held this concept of "ecumenism in time" as closely "correlated" to his program of neopatristic synthesis: see Matthew Baker, "The Correspondence between T.F. Torrance and Georges Florovsky (1950–1973)," *Participatio* 4 (2013): 287–323, at 320, http://www.tftorrance.org/journal/participatio_vol_4_2013.pdf.

in the Church is something greater, and something different, than memory alone, more than simple remembrance. Meeting in the context of Tradition is not a restoration—"restoration" always does violence to life. In any case, we cannot simply go back to the year 1054 and resolve anew the questions of those days. Both East and West have changed since then, and other questions now stand before us. Christian Tradition was split in the course of history. Now the task will be to restore its unity and completeness, and that should be the focus of theological dialogue. Meeting in the context of Tradition is a mutual process of coming to terms with the fullness of Tradition. No other way to a genuine reunion exists.

To many, such a broad program will seem impractical, unrealistic, and too "academic." For its implementation will clearly require a great deal of time and a huge mobilization of resources. Is it not possible to solve the problem more easily? In ecumenical circles there has long been talk concerning immediate "intercommunion" as the method of choice: Should we not just start with *communicatio in sacris*, that is, with the Eucharist, and postpone theological dialogue? Is it really necessary to strive toward a real unity in faith, apart from a formal agreement on some commonly accepted minimum, for example, the Nicene Creed, with the full freedom of interpretation of this minimum as well? Strange to say, this method is today sometimes proposed as a way of addressing the problem of reunification of Orthodoxy and Rome.[7] True, the "mini-

7. Florovsky is likely thinking here of the proposals of Fr. Nikolai Afanasiev (1893–1966).

mum" proposed in this case is much broader and more robust, but still with an undefined freedom of interpretation on issues such as apostolic succession, sacramental hierarchy, the mysteries, and a common *Credo*. Should we not start with the resumption of Eucharistic communion between the separated Churches, Orthodox and Roman, with no further "harmonization" in the doctrine of the faith? Strictly speaking, such a method is not new at all—it is the method of the *Unia*. The sterility and the ambiguity of this method have long been revealed in historical experience, and it would be strange to repeat it now, albeit in a new and more subtle format. The *Unia* does not provide any real unity. What is achieved is only the appearance of formal unity, but the "unified" parts do not coalesce. Pragmatism and relativism are injected into the realm of faith, along with a kind of indifference, on the pretext of theological pluralism. Of course it is true that unity in faith does not require uniformity in theology. A certain freedom in theological interpretation remains, but on condition of a living and organic coherence of these interpretions. And in the process we must strictly distinguish between the levels of dogma, doctrine, and theology. The distinctions are not easy to establish, for all these levels are linked to each other in the unity of ecclesial consciousness. In any case, there can be no room for pluralism in the dogmatic realm. Strictly speaking, such a formal scheme of "reunification" is unacceptable in present conditions because it is hopelessly out of date in spiritual and psychological terms, apart from being spiritually wrong. Our times, thank God, are characterized by a theological awakening, a new sensitivity to matters of faith, the search for a living fullness. Of course, this awakening has not embraced the whole of the Christian world. It must be hoped that, with God's help, it will grow. In this regard, theological dialogue may play the role of a kind of ferment.

There can be no doubt that the very fact of the meeting of two patriarchs—and the conditions that made it conceivable— speaks of the desire for unity. But what kind of "unity" is in question? It seems that the Orthodox side originally wished to bring other Christian confessions to the Palestinian meeting in order to make it completely "ecumenical" in composition. This did not materialize. Apparently the Vatican had in mind only the meeting of the two patriarchs. This limitation has profound ecclesiological meaning.[8] The theme of the relationship between Rome and Othodoxy is thereby extracted from the general ecumenical context on the grounds that it is unique. The ecclesiological emphasis becomes quite apparent. On the other hand, what was supposed to be discussed: "union" or "unity"? The distinction between these terms may appear artificial and arbitrary. However, it has recently been energetically insisted upon in some Orthodox circles that "Christian unity" is possible without "union." This is not just a question of terminology. The distinction of terms points to a division of tasks. Under the banner of "Christian unity," "collaboration" is implied, a cooperation in practical terms. This does not necessarily require "harmony" and "unity" in the faith, except in a

8. As noted in the introduction, Florovsky strongly disagreed with the proposal that the dialogue between Orthodoxy and Rome also include Protestant confessions.

very general sense. In this context the participation of other confessions becomes logical and desirable. In our dark and troubled times, this desire to create a sort of united "Christian front" for direct action is understandable, and one can even sympathize with this desire. But it is nevertheless necessary to make at least two substantial reservations. First of all, it is not surprising that in today's environment the emphasis is often is transferred to the opposition of "belief" and "unbelief"—it is a vital contemporary theme. But often there is a tacit, but no less dangerous, substitution of "religion in general" for Christianity, and the *content of the faith* is relegated to the background. In this perspective, the differences between separated Christians lose practical importance, and the question of unity is reduced to the psychological or the political planes. In reality, however, the power of Christian unity resides precisely in the unity of faith, within the Unity of the Church. In the second place, no matter how desirable Christian "cooperation" in particular cases and within certain limits might be, it does not lead to a real unity, and even overshadows the very theme of "unity"—*unity in the One Church*. Strictly speaking, Christian "cooperation" is, in the final analysis, an inevitably ambiguous undertaking. "Cooperation" can serve the cause of Christian unity only when it is inwardly linked to the search for "unity," that is, for *Unity in the Church*. Otherwise, it can easily lose its distinguishing Christian character and become a hindrance to "unity." This danger is very real.

The Palestinian meeting of the Patriarchs—of the new and the old Rome, long and still divided—is, in any case, a timely *reminder*, in fact a double reminder, of the fact of separation

69

and of the task of unity. A reminder and *a summons*. . . . This is only the beginning of the way. In the apt expression of St. Basil the Great, "the beginning of the way is not yet the way." The question now is how the voice of the Church will respond to this reminder and summons. The subject of Rome is once again brought before Orthodox consciousness. For some, Rome is a Church, even though a "separated Church." For others, Rome is simply outside the Church. There are similar disagreements among Roman theologians, with a variety of nuances. This question requires a thorough theological elaboration. The question of Rome is a question of ecclesiology.

Orthodoxy in our time is being summoned to theological work. Only this will reveal the universal nature of Orthodoxy.

"The watchman said, The morning cometh, but it is still night."

Cambridge, Mass.

Afterword:
The Dawn of
Expectation

◇◇◇◇◇◇◇◇◇◇◇◇◇◇◇

Walter Cardinal Kasper

The commemoration of the fiftieth anniversary since the historic meeting between Pope Paul VI and Ecumenical Patriarch Athenagoras of Constantinople in the Holy City of Jerusalem on January 5–6, 1964, is first of all an occasion to give thanks to the almighty and ever-merciful God, whose Holy Spirit inspired this blessed beginning of a new and promising age in the relations between the sister Churches of Rome and Constantinople after the long night of separation, silence, and expectation.

The moving exchange of letters, messages, and discourses that initiated, attended, and followed this extraordinary meeting provide ample and clear evidence that it was the intention of the heads of both churches to realize the prayer of our Lord and Savior expressed on the eve of his death that all may be one. They were aware of the difficulties that lay ahead along the way to full communion. Nonetheless they were convinced that it is imperative for them, as it is for all Christians worthy of their name, to overcome differences and dissents, as well as

71

to break down the barriers of the past in order to walk in truth on the path of reconciliation, forgiveness, and love. In this sense they discerned the dawn of a new bright and blessed day, where future generations communicate from the same chalice of the body and the blood of our Savior, working together as brothers and sisters for unity and peace in our world.

Today, fifty years later, we gratefully acknowledge that with the help of God's Spirit we were able to take many steps in truth and love toward the unity our Lord wants for His unique body. Yet we also have to confess that on many occasions we fell behind His divine will, gave scandal to the world with our disunion, and damaged that most holy cause: namely, the shared preaching of the Gospel, which our world so urgently needs and desires.

Therefore, it is with shared faith and fraternal love that we celebrate the May 2014 meeting in Jerusalem between Pope Francis and Ecumenical Patriarch Bartholomew. We pray that this new meeting will be not only a clear and convincing confirmation of the intentions of the first encounter but also a powerful new impulse to advance on the way of fraternal dialogue and cooperation in order to reach full communion, which respects the legitimate differences of both of our traditions while fully uniting us in the one apostolic faith and in one Eucharistic celebration for the praise of the most Holy Trinity and for the sake of our world, which urgently needs us as credible witnesses of unity and peace.

There is no time to lose, but it is high time to fulfill what God's Spirit initiated fifty years ago.

CONTRIBUTORS

Metropolitan John (Zizioulas) of Pergamon studied in Thessaloniki and Athens, pursuing graduate research at Harvard with Fr. Georges Florovsky. He taught systematic theology at the universities of Edinburgh and Glasgow, as well as London and Thessaloniki. He has represented the Ecumenical Patriarchate in prominent capacities at the World Council of Churches as well as in international theological dialogues with the Anglican and Roman Catholic Churches, chairing the latter since 2006. He has served as chairman of the Academy of Athens and authored many influential theological and ecological publications.

John Chryssavgis is Archdeacon of the Ecumenical Throne and a clergyman of the Greek Orthodox Archdiocese of America, where he serves as theological advisor in the Office of Inter-Orthodox Ecumenical and Interfaith Relations. He studied in Athens and Oxford, as well as taught in Sydney and Boston. The author of numerous books and articles on Orthodox theology, spirituality, and ecology, he edited three volumes containing the select writings of Ecumenical Patriarch Bartholomew (Fordham University Press, 2010–12). He lives in Harpswell, Maine.

Brian E. Daley, S.J., a graduate of Fordham College and Oxford University, is the Catherine F. Huisking Professor of Theology at the University of Notre Dame. His interests are focused on the Christology, Trinitarian theology, and eschatology of the early Church. He has been a member of the North American Orthodox-Catholic Consultation since 1981 and is now its Catholic Executive Secretary. In 2012, he was awarded the Ratzinger Prize in Theology by the Ratzinger Foundation in Rome, and in 2013 was given the Johannes Quasten Medal by the School of Theology at the Catholic University of America.

Protopresbyter Georges Florovsky (1893–1979) was a leading Orthodox theologian, philosopher, historian, and ecumenist of the twentieth century. He taught patristics at Institut Saint-Serge in Paris (1926–48), St. Vladimir's Seminary (1948–54), Harvard University and Holy Cross Greek Orthodox Seminary (1955–64), as well as Princeton University and Princeton Theological Seminary (1965–79). A theological authority throughout the Orthodox and ecumenical world, Florovsky was the major architect of the neopatristic movement and a founding member of the World Council of Churches.

Matthew Baker is a PhD candidate in systematic theology at Fordham University, currently writing a dissertation on neopatristic theology and modern philosophical hermeneutics. A presbyter of the Greek Orthodox Archdiocese of America (Metropolis of Boston), he is presently adjunct professor at Hellenic College/Holy Cross Greek Orthodox School of Theology.

He is codirector with Seraphim Danckaert of the Fr. Georges Florovsky Orthodox Theological Society at Princeton.

Walter Cardinal Kasper is president emeritus of the Pontifical Council for Promoting Christian Unity, where he served as president from 2001 to 2010. He taught dogmatic theology at the University of Tübingen and the Westphalian University of Münster. He has led many official delegations of the Vatican to the Ecumenical Patriarchate. A member of the International Theological Commission, his books include *Searching for Christian Unity: 40 Years of Unitatis Redintegratio.*

ORTHODOX CHRISTIANITY AND CONTEMPORARY THOUGHT

*George E. Demacopoulos
and Aristotle Papanikolaou*

SERIES EDITORS

Ecumenical Patriarch Bartholomew, *In the World, Yet Not of the World: Social and Global Initiatives of Ecumenical Patriarch Bartholomew.* Edited by John Chryssavgis. Foreword by Jose Manuel Barroso.

Ecumenical Patriarch Bartholomew, *Speaking the Truth in Love: Theological and Spiritual Exhortations of Ecumenical Patriarch Bartholomew.* Edited by John Chryssavgis. Foreword by Dr. Rowan Williams, Archbishop of Canterbury.

Ecumenical Patriarch Bartholomew, *On Earth as in Heaven: Ecological Vision and Initiatives of Ecumenical Patriarch Bartholomew.* Edited by John Chryssavgis. Foreword by His Royal Highness, the Duke of Edinburgh.

George E. Demacopoulos and Aristotle Papaniklaou (eds.), *Orthodox Constructions of the West.*

John Chryssavgis and Bruce V. Foltz (eds.), *Toward an Ecology of Transfiguration: Orthodox Christian Perspectives on Environment, Nature, and Creation.* Foreword by Bill McKibben. Prefatory Letter by Ecumenical Patriarch Bartholomew.

Lucian N. Leustean (ed.), *Orthodox Christianity and Nationalism in Nineteenth-Century Southeastern Europe.*

John Chryssavgis (ed.), *Dialogue of Love: Breaking the Silence of Centuries.* Contributions by Brian E. Daley, S.J., and Georges Florovsky.